Teaching Spirits

Teaching Spirits

Understanding

Native American

Religious Traditions

JOSEPH EPES BROWN

with Emily Cousins

OXFORD
UNIVERSITY PRESS

2001

OXFORD
UNIVERSITY PRESS

Oxford   New York
Athens   Auckland   Bangkok   Bogotá   Buenos Aires   Cape Town
Dar es Salaam   Delhi   Florence   Hong Kong   Istanbul   Karachi
Kolkata   Kuala Lumpur   Madras   Madrid   Melbourne   Mexico City   Nairobi
Paris   São Paulo   Shanghai   Singapore   Taipei   Tokyo   Toronto   Warsaw

and associated companies in
Berlin   Ibadan

Copyright © 2001 by Joseph Epes Brown

Published by Oxford University Press, Inc.
198 Madison Avenue, New York, New York 10016

Oxford is a registered trademark of Oxford University Press

Library of Congress Cataloging-in-Publication Data
Brown, Joseph Epes.
Teaching spirits : understanding Native American religious traditions /
Joseph Epes Brown with Emily Cousins.
    p.   cm.
ISBN 0-19-513875-9
1. Indians of North America—Religion.   2. Indian mythology—North America.
3. Indians of North America—Rites and ceremonies.
I. Cousins, Emily.   II. Title.
E98.R3 B753 2001
299'.7—dc21   00-044072

9 8 7 6 5 4 3 2 1

Printed in the United States of America
on acid-free paper

ACKNOWLEDGMENTS

WE WOULD LIKE TO THANK Celeste River and Philip Jones, two of Joseph Brown's graduate students and friends, for their valuable contributions, suggestions, and class notes. Rodney Frey, a former student and colleague, also shared his memories. Donald Good Voice generously included his reflections on studying with Joseph.

Literary agent Susan Bergholz contributed sound advice, Professor Ewert Cousins gave endless encouragement, and Daniel Scott offered support and inspiration. Friend and colleague Peter Nabokov provided essential suggestions and insights.

We also thank the many students who sent class notes, recollections, art work, and contributions, including Rucina Ballinger, Julia Becker, Joe Campbell, Sherry Dingman, Richard Feldman, Woody Kipp, Richard Manning, Susie Lindbergh Miller, Malcolm O'Leary, Nancy Rey, and Charles Stephens.

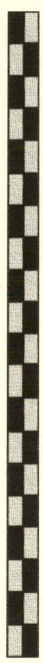

CONTENTS

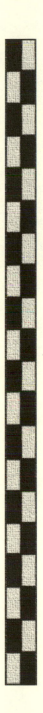

How You Speak Could Change the World

I AM A CHIPPEWA-CREE from the Rocky Boy Reservation. I am forty-two years old. My dad, John Gilbert Meyers, was born in 1932 and pretty much was raised traditional. He raised us eleven kids with the old traditional style of living, of showing respect, of not being too boastful, of taking things real slow, and of respecting the things that we don't understand.

Meeting Joe was a really good experience for me. It was during the seventies when Indian people, especially my generation, were going through what you would call an identity crisis. Many of us were pushed off the reservations to seek better education and higher learning, but there was a sacrifice we had to make for this. The sacrifice, which I made partially to be in a place of higher learning, was to put aside our traditional upbringing and our traditional beliefs. We had to become aggressive and boisterous, become like the non-Indian who runs the system. We had been led to believe ever since kindergarten that the old ways were done for, that they had no meaning, no monetary or economic value. All the way up until graduation from high school, we were told that the traditional way wasn't of any consequence and that we were something that had to be turned around and remade. That had a tremendous effect on our self-esteem; that's where our identity crisis began.

When I first met Joe, I felt like I was going down a wrong road. I was kind of like a fake, a carbon copy. I guess I was shooting for that ultimate goal of being a WASP. That was unrealistic, but that was what my dad and other people wanted for us. They didn't really want us to be WASPs, but they wanted a better life for their children. My mother, my dad, their relatives, they grew up in an age of terrible poverty when the Depression was going full blast. Their grandparents were alive at a time when the U.S. government outlawed their religion and their language. They grew up in an era when it was frightening to be Indian, to be traditional. It was a matter of life and death for them.

But Joe made me and my generation realize that there was something valuable in our old traditions. We thought our traditional religion was something to be ashamed of, something we had to do on the sly. Joe made it okay; he made it seem like it was our basic human right. I guess Joe was a catalyst for us. We were jumping from one world to another world, but there was no bridge. So Joe became the bridge that made the connection. Suddenly we were whole again. It was good.

I was trying to figure out these two worlds when I met Joe. I had to choose what classes to take, and, as I was looking through the University of Montana catalogue, I saw that there was a Native American religion course being offered by this Joseph Epes Brown. I asked around about him, and people said they really enjoyed his classes and got a lot out of them. At first some of the Native American students were offended that here was this white man talking about Indian religion. They wondered what he knew about Indians, but, once they took the class and participated in his classroom, their attitudes changed dramatically. They realized that his approach was different, the way he handled students was different; it was more humane. He made us feel like we were the teachers and that he was there to learn from us.

So I made a point to go visit him in his office. The reception I got was overwhelming to me, because he treated me so well, so warmly. I was never treated like that by other instructors. They didn't treat me like a human being; they treated me like a number. But Joe told me to sit down, and he brought me a cup of tea. When he got me all comfortable and situated, then he asked, "What tribe are you? What's your name?" It was so unusual, because I was used to a type of structured interview. He wanted to forget that for a while and get to know each other on a human basis; then we could do the required thing at the end. He showed me his office, showed me his buffalo skull and paintings by his student, Arthur Amiotte. He showed me everything, and it made me feel like a special person. I thought, "This man radiates kindness." So, right then and there I decided I would take his class.

When I went to his first class, I was surprised that there were more non-Indians than there were Indians. Some of the non-Indians were antagonistic and close-minded. Some of them were trying to make him stumble over his knowledge of Native Americans and his experiences with Black Elk. They were after the power situation. They wanted to know if Joe had any of the spiritual power that Black Elk had, which is so superficial. That's not why Joe was with Black Elk. He was there for the knowledge that could be shared with the coming generations, but they didn't see it that way; they saw it in terms of what was in it for them. Joe never got offended, though. He would give a straight answer, an answer from the heart, and it satisfied them because they wouldn't ask the same question again. He always made them feel that it was okay to have such questions.

His classes guided some of the Indian people in the gray area who chose to be in the plastic world. He guided them back and made them realize, "Hey, there's beauty in your way. There's beauty in your traditions; there's beauty in your culture. Don't throw it away." I remember him saying in class, "You have a beautiful way about you, you have a beautiful background behind you. People in your tribe years ago, they had a social structure that was so humane, so democratic, so pure that it couldn't be improved upon, because it gave everybody equal right, equal opportunities for women, for children, for old people. It was so great," he said. "Hang on to that. That's going to be more valuable to you than these books, than money, than credit cards." And it's so true. He gave us so much value, so much to look forward to. He gave us hope.

He taught in such a manner that you came away feeling that you'd taught yourself. He let us find our own answers. It was as if he said, "Here are your questions, and here are your answers all around you." He never acted like an expert, a know-it-all, or a guru; he was a guide. A lot of times he would let me or another Native American student answer a question if it was directed to a specific tribe. If the student felt uncomfortable, he would answer. Some of us weren't able to express ourselves as well as he did, but he made us feel like a part of the class, like we had something to contribute to the teaching.

One time he gave us the assignment to do something in the old traditional manner. That sparked something I had forgotten since I was a little kid. When Joe gave us that assignment, my wife and I were expecting our first child, Sweet Grass Man, so I decided to make an old traditional cradle board. I killed the deer, got the hide, and the meat, then I got a tree for the board and made the rawhide, buckskin ties. My grandmother on my mom's side, she helped me tan the hide. The only thing I used that wasn't traditional was the tacks for the back; I used brass tacks. I put it together, and I took it to my mom and asked her if it was correct. My mother, my grandmother, everybody had a hand in this little project that he gave us.

"Yeah," my mom said, "you only left one thing out." What I had forgotten was what you see nowadays called dream catchers. This was even before anyone knew what dream catchers were all about. My mom said, "You gotta get one of those and put it right where the baby's heart is so nothing bad gets in. When they sleep at night, anything bad gets caught in that net." So I fixed it up. I took it back to her, and she said, "Yeah, that's good. Now you can paint the cradleboard." So I asked her what I should paint on it.

She said, "Well, what are the two things that we experience each day?"

"I don't know," I said.

"Well, what do you do when you go to bed?"

"I go to sleep."

"What is it then?"

"It's dark."

"Well, then dark and light," she said. "Put those together." So I got dark blue for one side of the cradle board and yellow for the other side, for day and night. This child within this cradle board will be protected day and night.

Then she said, "What kind of protection are you going to give this child?" I thought of the porcupine, because the porcupine is slow, but it gets where it wants to go. It is harmless, it doesn't bother, it doesn't attack, it's not aggressive. But, if you attack it, you get hurt pretty bad. So I used the quill and the hairs from the porcupine and tied it on to the cradle board, along with some figurines of horses and lightning. I wanted my son to be protected by the Thunders and by the horse spirit. The horse was important to me at that time, and still is, because the horse is strong, the horse chose to be with man, and the horse chose to work for man. That's why I put the horse on the cradle board.

I got it all complete and showed it to my mom again, and she said, "Yeah, that's correct. But next time," she said, "use the floral design of the old Cree style. That way you don't get into the situation of what powers are around. The old floral design is a safe thing to do for children and cradle boards."

I completed the project and brought it to class and turned it in to Joe. He looked at it, and he said, "That's good. What was the question?" Right there I knew I answered it. It was so great. My eyes were opened, my mind was opened. A whole new door was opened up for me. That's how he did it. That's how he affected people. It was such a good experience because the whole family did it, from my grandmother, to my mother, to my dad, to me, to the kids. We all had a hand in it, and that was just one little project.

It was like the old social order we used to have years ago, before we were forced to adopt this new style of life. We knew we were all connected. We all did things for each other, we all shared something. That's how we were able to have those close-knit extended families. Even when we were alone, we were never alone. Maybe we had a shirt that our cousin had made or our auntie had made or our grandma had made for us, or moccasins some relative had made for us. That's what we are losing now. We are losing that close-knit, extended family. I couldn't really say we are losing it; it is just taking a different shape and form nowadays. It is more commercial than it used to be a long time ago when it was love and compassion we had for each other. Now it's more like, "Well, we'll do it for you, but it's going to cost you." We're getting into that situation now.

Joe is a strong believer in the traditional ways. I remember his son, Sasha, lived with the Berber over in Morocco, and he brought back stuff for his dad. There was a whole set of knives—they were like daggers—made by the Berber; they made the steel and fashioned the blades. One of the knives reminded me of how my Grandma, like most of the old timers, used to cure headaches by cutting people's temples. She would cut the skin, put some medicine in there, and close it back up. And people would stop having headaches. I told Joe about that and said a knife like that would be really handy. But, you see, in the old traditional ways, you don't give people knives. It's bad luck. What you do is throw the knife at their feet and say, "Oh, look. A knife." I forgot all about that, but later, when I was getting ready to leave, something landed at my feet and I said, "Hey look! A knife." Joe respected the old ways to the point that he didn't want to wish bad luck on me or anybody, so he did that. And I still have that knife.

Joe had an impact not only on myself personally, but on a lot of the Native American people he met, because he shared his knowledge freely with us. Not once did he ask for anything in return. One time he said Black Elk was that way. Black Elk freely gave Joe knowledge of things that were important, things that maybe Joe didn't understand right away but that later he grew to understand. When he had that understanding, he shared it with us, and that validated our traditional beliefs and ceremonies. It let us love one another, which is important because there is a lot of violence on the reservations, a lot of self-directed violence. Joe helped us see that ceremonies that make the connection among the earth, the Creator, and ourselves can center us. As Black Elk said, any place on the earth can be the center of the universe. Joe helped us realize that you can find the center anywhere as long as you are centered, as long as your heart, your mind, and your soul are centered. That is what matters.

I'll admit there are a lot of Native American people my age who have slipped into that mode of denying who they are. They get lost in that plastic world, the fast-food world, where everything is instant gratification. The old traditions, the old way of life is difficult, but it is lasting. People say, "You want to go back to the old tipi, the old days, and wear breech cloth and feathers." But no, that's not what we want, that's not what our generation is about. Our generation is finding out what's important, what's real, what the mores are that will help us survive as a people. Our choice is not to live in the tipi, not to ride horses and to wear buckskins, but to find something that's lasting. We have to live in this modern world facing realities like radical extremists and diseases—both old diseases that are making a comeback and new diseases that are related to modern life. There are also the consequences that come from mining, from desecrating burial sites. We can't put our heads in the sand. We want our kids, our next generation, to face the world head on, but to still retain the traditional background that they come from.

We especially want them to remember the old timers, the old people who made the sacrifices they did so that we have a place to live. Sure, we call them the reservations, that's fine, but they're home.

One of the realities our young people have to face is that at least the reservations are a stronghold for us, a base where we can always feel comfortable and practice our religion a lot more freely than we did fifty years ago. I was lucky enough to meet a lot of those old timers, and they said they used to hide their old religious articles, their bundles. They had to do their ceremonies in secret, because the government was so afraid that we were going to have another uprising. The government didn't want those kinds of religious activities to happen, even though those ceremonies were intended for mankind. When we pray, we pray not just for Native Americans, but for all mankind. At the time, I didn't understand, but now I do. It is heart wrenching, because I think, "Oh, if only our people could've practiced our religion, maybe things would be a little different today."

But things are not different, and that's what we want our kids to realize. We have camps for the kids from Rocky Boy and neighboring tribes where they can learn about themselves, about the old traditional values. We are not encouraging young people to dress in buckskin and feathers. That's not the point. The point is to enhance the values—what's important to them as Indian people, such as honesty and hard work. We teach them the old traditional survival techniques, how to find water, set up camp, hunt, tan hides, cook, and share the duties with the women. We teach them about sweats—how the sweats tie into our survival. We make sure that when we hunt, we hunt in an appropriate manner, that we don't squander meat, we use everything that we kill, and we treat everything with respect.

I also go into teachers' classrooms around Rocky Boy and Havre to talk about the values our traditionals used to have, how they affect us today, and how they should be carried on. But what a lot of non-Indian teachers find hard to accept is that the mores and values we had are so connected with religion. They feel uncomfortable because of problems with the separation of church and state. But we say, "Hey, that's the way of life we had and still have. If you want me to talk about that or our personal beliefs, you are going to have to accept that." There is not distinction between religion and every day life in our way. We take that for granted. It's just the way of life we have. In the morning we get up, the first thing we do is offer thanks. In the evening before we go to bed, we offer thanks. We don't think that is religion; we just think that's the way it's supposed to be. That's the way we were taught to live, to respect creation, to respect ourselves.

That lack of distinction between religion and daily life is a problem for a lot of non-Indians.

There are so many of these issues to face, it's no wonder our young people are confused, disoriented, don't know which path to take. I find it strange that now non-Indians are more interested in our old values than our young people. People are searching, because they've lost something through the emphasis on materialism. They are finding out that materials will not save their souls. It's ironic, because at one time we were thought of as devils and everything about us was evil. We are now just getting out of that shadow, in part because people like Joe validated our religion, said it was just as valid as Islam, Buddhism, and Christianity.

Our ancestors couldn't speak, so Joe spoke for them. Our old timers, they always admonished us, "Be careful how you talk. Choose your words carefully, because how you speak could change the world." It is true. Joe changed worlds. He changed our world. He brought some love and some light into this world, a world that to me and to our old people was full of darkness and uncertainty, full of hatred, full of hurt. Now, because of Joe's teaching and this book, there are some good things to look forward to, some good things, some powerful things.

Rocky Boy Reservation   Don Good Voice
Box Elder, Montana
April, 2000

THE OLD FORESTRY BUILDING where Joseph Brown held many of his classes at the University of Montana was home to Bertha the Moose. In a warm, stuffy classroom on the second floor, Bertha's huge head hung above the podium where Joseph taught his courses on Native American religious traditions. Upon entering the classroom, Joseph would never fail to nod a greeting to Bertha. During his lectures, he would often stop in midsentence, turn, and look up to her with a kind smile and gently touch her large nose or whisper something to her. Students would lean forward, trying to catch what this gentleman with the patrician features and the New England accent had to say to a moose. With a twinkle in his eye, Joseph would smile and say, "I need some help with the lecture today, and Bertha can help me." When he wasn't sure about something, he would turn and ask Bertha, "Isn't that right?" or "What do you think, Bertha?"

Every year, the forestry students would take Bertha to the Annual Forester's Ball, where she reigned as the school mascot and belle. The classroom during that week was bleak and empty, her presence sorely missed. Out of habit, Joseph would turn to consult Bertha, only to be faced by her darker head shape, stenciled on the pale green walls over the years. Everyone was glad when she returned to pre-side once again over Joseph and his words.

Joseph's relationship with Bertha modeled for his students a deep sense of respect: respect for animals, as well as respect for the Native American religious traditions that hold animals in high esteem. Whether it was with a moose, a Plains pipe, or a young child who attended a lecture with a parent, Joseph quietly conveyed that sense of respect for the complexity and the dignity of Native traditions.

This book carries on his teaching tradition and sustains the quality of respect he inspired.

Comprising his articles, class notes, and lectures, this book offers a thematic introduction to Native North American religious traditions. Joseph valued story telling and the oral transmission of knowledge, but he also appreciated the power of the written word. This book is a unique interweaving of both and includes what Joseph put down on paper as well as what he said. It draws from stories, scholarship, images, and personal experiences to build an understanding of the traditions that continue to thrive in Native America today. It also reminds us that we are surrounded by beings like Bertha, who are willing to teach us if we will only listen.

Joseph's engagement with Native American traditions stretches back into his childhood, when he listened to the stories of Abenaki elders near his family's home in Maine. During World War II, Joseph read *Black Elk Speaks*, the story, as recounted to John Neihardt, of a young Oglala Lakota holy man's experience of the years just before the reservation era. This book inspired him to buy an old Ford truck, convert it into a camper, and head west to find Black Elk. He finally located Black Elk in a migrant camp in Nebraska, where his family was digging potatoes. Joseph quietly entered Black Elk's tent, not at all sure of his reception. He sat beside the old man in silence and lit a pipe for the two to share. When the pipe was finished, Black Elk turned to him and said, "What took you so long? I've been waiting for you."

Joseph lived with Black Elk's family for a year on the Pine Ridge Reservation and listened as Black Elk passed on the teachings of the seven sacred rites of the Oglala. Joseph also developed friendships with Lakota elders, such as the venerated Yuwipi man Little Warrior and others who had fought at the Battle of the Little Bighorn 1876 and witnessed the Massacre at Wounded Knee in 1890. In 1950 Black Elk died, and in 1953 Joseph published *The Sacred Pipe: Black Elk's Account of the Seven Rites of the Oglala Sioux*.

In the years after his work with Black Elk, Joseph continued to travel to reservations around the country. Poverty and the effects of prejudice were rampant on reservations, and Joseph was disgusted with the ignorance and the disrespect that characterized many white people's actions toward Native Americans. He came to believe that educating non-Indians was one way to combat the racism. Joseph and his wife spent many years teaching Native American traditions, World Religions, and Humanities at Verde Valley School, an innovative private high school in Sedona, Arizona.

After some time, however, Joseph realized that, in order to effectively communicate Native American experience to a wide audience, he needed the tools recognized by the non-Native society: graduate degrees. He turned to academia with reluctance, knowing that few departments showed respect for Native cultures. He started out in a master's program in anthropology at the University of New Mexico but was immediately discouraged when, at the reception for new students, guests had to wear name tags attached to human bones from the department's forays into Native burial sites. He left academia after a year and returned to teaching. He finally finished his master's degree years later at Stanford University. In 1969 he found a nurturing environment with the preeminent religious historian Åke Hultkrantz at the University of Stockholm, where he received a doctoral degree in both anthropology and the history of religions.

As he began to look for teaching jobs at the university level, he realized his options were limited. Joseph hoped to receive a position in a religion department, but few universities considered teaching Native traditions in their course offerings. Most disciplines still referred to Native Americans in the past tense, if they referred to them at all. Joseph, however, wanted to show students that Native American traditions were alive and dynamic and should be considered among the world religions. In 1970 Indiana University gave Joseph the rare opportunity to do just that by offering him a position in the religious studies department. Within this innovative department, he taught Native American religious traditions to classes of between 500 and 600 students. Two years later, he accepted an invitation to join the religious studies department at the University of Montana. Until his retirement from University of Montana in 1989, Joseph was able to help draw the study of Native American religious traditions into their rightful place of honor and respect within American higher education.

In 1989 Joseph was diagnosed with Alzheimer's Disease. Letters from teachers and readers requesting course outlines and reading lists continued to arrive at Joseph's home. Former students repeatedly asked his family if they were publishing his notes and writings. In response, Joseph's family decided to compile a book that could help pass on his teachings. His wife, Elenita Brown, a dancer and designer, had assisted Joseph in editing *The Sacred Pipe* and had shared his travels to reservations. His daughter, Marina Brown Weatherly, an artist and writer, was a former student of his and is presently working on an oral history of the Crow woman Susie Yellowtail. Together, Joseph's wife and his daughter began brainstorming ways to share his work with more people.

I had first met Joseph as a young girl when I visited his ranch in Montana with my family. After I majored in religion and art history in college, I looked forward to studying with Joseph in the future. I was working as a writer and editor when I learned of his illness, and I contacted Elenita to ask if she needed help compiling his work. I was invited to move to their ranch in western Montana, where the three of us began designing the format for this book.

Although Joseph taught numerous subjects, including comparative religions, Islam, sacred art, humanities, and ecology, we decided to limit the subject of this book to Native North American traditions. We began by gathering the many writings in Joseph's files. As we read through them, we discovered that they were telling two stories. The first was the story of Native American religious traditions. The second was the story of Joseph's teaching. His classroom lecture notes told us how he structured his classes, what themes he emphasized, and which examples he used to illustrate his points. His articles told us about his writing style and content. The transcriptions of talks he gave at universities and conferences told us how he wove humor, personal experience, and humility into discussions of Native American religious traditions.

Since we wanted the book to reflect Joseph's teaching, we thought it was essential to hear from his former students, so we invited them to send us their notes from his lectures. These, too, had a story to tell. They told us about topics that Joseph would simply refer to in his own notes, since he was so familiar with the material. The student notes rounded out Joseph's notes, for, when put side by side, they completed the cycle from speaker to listener.

Once we gathered all of Joseph's writings and his students' notes, we began to consider how they could be drawn together. We quickly realized that the material had an organizing structure already embedded within it. In most of his writings and talks, Joseph preferred to discuss Native American religious traditions by theme rather than by cultural regions such as Southwest or Woodlands. Even when Joseph focused his courses around the Plains or the Southwest, it was the central themes that shaped and moved his discussions. Joseph thought that regional designations ignored the dynamic flow of cultural exchange and that the depth of religious experience was more engaging than geographical categories.

He observed that, within the great multiplicity of Native American tribes, there are certain shared themes that are central to their religious world views: sacred time and place, the power of language and art, the importance of reciprocal relationships with the natural world, and the transformative process of ritual. The same thematic pattern emerged from the corpus of his notes and writings. We decided to honor the design that Joseph himself had so often chosen. Each chapter of this book represents one of these themes.

With this outline in place, I began the process of organizing the writings according to these themes. For instance, I put a short article on the sacred power of language with the references to oral traditions from Joseph's class notes. A talk that described Apaches stories of place became a part of the section on sacred geography. Deciding where material should go required careful attention to Joseph's method and repeated cross-referencing through all of his work. For example, while the ceremonial hunting of a deer for its hide could be a part of the discussion of ritual, Joseph used it as an example of the sacred dimensions of the artistic process. Because of the unified nature of Native American traditional culture, it can be difficult to assign cultural dynamics to fragmented Western categories. To steer through these interconnections, I carefully followed the map of Joseph's own work.

Once Joseph's thoughts and writings had been organized according to his thematic structure, each chapter had to be crafted into a whole. This was a challenging task, since I was working with the differently textured threads of written articles, oral transmission, notes, and memories. I began each chapter by selecting a core article or lecture. This became the spool around which the related threads were wrapped, each new example from class or article adding another layer to the thickening skein.

The different threads still had to be woven together, and holes had to be filled. While some of Joseph's notes were extensive, some consisted of brief phrases used to jog his memory. For instance, lecture notes on the Navajo perception of language included the following thoughts:

xxii

> Words don't just describe, *They Create*
> Force which animates everything in the world:
>   "Indwelling Wind Spirit"
> Capacity to shape wind = Act of Creativity
>   Thus the power of human word
>   Babies same category as animals until they talk

For this type of notation, I added the syntax necessary to tie the thoughts together. Other notes listed elements of a ritual ceremony, such as the following on the Ojibwa Medewewin ceremony:

> Candidates: one who had been ill or
> dreamed he should go through
> Midé priest
> Preparations—Gifts
> *Mi'gis* worn by candidate
> *Wayan* Med. otter bag
> Preliminary instructions in Wigwam
> Songs taught secrets of the Society
> related to the 4 degrees
> Sweat Bath

Joseph did not always write descriptions of each of these steps, since he knew them so well by heart. When this occurred, I would turn to Joseph's library for the books he had read and underlined so that I could fill in the details. In some of his notes, Joseph referred to stories he liked to tell during a lecture, such as the "Gopher story" or the "Black Hills Race Track story." If I could not find a version of the story Joseph had written, I would ask former students to tell it to me. While it may seem that this process is one step removed from Joseph's work, it honors something he took very seriously: passing on knowledge through oral transmission.

Another type of gap remained to be filled, and that was one of time. Joseph made a point of telling his classes about the struggles that Native Americans face in maintaining access to sacred land.

Since his illness, however, it was not possible for him to remain informed, so we decided to update some of the relevant information. In the chapter on ritual, for instance, I added references to Senator Daniel Inouye's efforts to bring the Native American Religious Freedom Act before the U.S. Congress in 1995. In the chapter on sacred land, I included a discussion of the Sweet Grass Hills, an area in North Central Montana that is sacred to several tribes but is in danger of being mined for gold. We chose this site not only because it embodies many of the issues Joseph spoke about in relation to other places but also because it is close to his own homeland.

In the years since Joseph retired in 1989, there has been enormous growth in publications by Native Americans. We thought it was important to represent this growing body of resources, since Joseph would have welcomed the shift from whites writing most of the books about Native Americans to Native Americans writing about themselves. I used quotes from recent sources to illustrate some of Joseph's ideas. For instance, when Joseph spoke about the interrelatedness of humans and animals, I turned to a book entitled *Messengers of the Wind: Native American Women Tell Their Life Stories* (Ballantine Books, 1995) for a quote from Virginia Poole, a Seminole tribal member, in which she talks about how animals and humans used to trade places. My goal in adding quotes was to augment and underscore Joseph's thinking, not to distract the reader from his original intention. To help ensure that all additions I made were consistent with the body of Joseph's work, Elenita and Marina edited every draft of each chapter, focusing on content, flow, and, most important, authenticity.

Just as this book was going to publication, Joseph died at his home in Stevensville, Montana on September 19, 2000. More than ever, we were pleased to know that his teaching would continue to live on. We knew this book could not encompass all of Joseph's thought, nor could it include all there was to say about Native American religious traditions. We simply wanted to be certain that what could be included here is, to the best of our knowledge, true to Joseph's scholarship, personal experience, and story.

Stevensville, Montana   E. C.
April, 2000

Teaching Spirits

ONE

Back to Back

THERE IS AN unprecedented interest today in all facets of the Native North American heritage. It is especially significant that this interest is shared by Native Americans and non-Native Americans alike. Native American participation in traditional ceremonies is growing, and many non-Natives are beginning to see beyond superficial stereotypes in their understanding of Native American traditions. Underlying many Native Americans' renewed interest in their own traditions is their increasing disenchantment with a society that for centuries has been presented as the ultimate model of true civilization. Paralleling the disenchantment of Native Americans is the non-Native Americans' questioning of many of the basic premises of their own civilization. Both Indian and non-Indian are engaged in a quest for the roots of lost heritages now increasingly understood to be essential if we are to reorient our cultures and lives toward values that express real human nature.

The quest for these roots has become compelling because we are faced today with a pervasive process of detraditionalization or despiritualization on a global scale. The world has been experiencing this process in a cumulative manner for many centuries. Exceedingly complex historical causes beyond the scope of this book are no doubt responsible. As this process of detraditionalization has proceeded, its influence has demanded that the basic premises and orientations of our society be reevaluated.

Detraditionalization has had an impact on the integrity of virtually all Native American traditions or lifeways. Frequently, when

Native Americans make sincere attempts to adjust to or acculturate within mainstream society, they become involved in a process of diminishing returns or reach dead ends with regard to acquiring a meaningful quality of life. This disenchantment has inspired many Native Americans to reintegrate into the sacred ways of their traditions. The ground-breaking work of the empowerment movements of the 1960s is now beginning to take shape. On almost all reservations, neglected or abandoned rites and ceremonies are being brought out into the open, relearned, and participated in once again. As tribal control of schools slowly increases, more children are learning Native languages, stories, crafts, and other skills necessary for carrying on their traditions.

For some non-Native Americans, on the other hand, an increasing malaise has led to a mood of reassessment. We live under the force of a pervasive, materialistic outlook that spreads essentially from the Western world. Many people have begun to take a backward look at "progress," that concept that for so long has been an unquestioned quasi-religious dogma in non-Native culture. Longing for a lost, more real world of true freedom, many people have turned in every possible direction for alternative answers. It is not surprising that as the global ecological dilemma intensifies, many non-Natives are drawn to Native American traditions that express rich spiritual relationships with *this* continent. This sense of connectedness is but one of many aspects that point to the relevance of Native American values to a contemporary world in crisis.

In the rush to find answers in a dehumanizing world, however, there is the danger that non-Natives will adopt Native American traditions without fully understanding them. Because of their disillusionment and the spiritual impoverishment of their own religious traditions, and because they are unable in these times to understand the true nature of their own traditions, many non-Natives have no real criteria for discrimination, evaluation, and eventual choice. Sometimes the motivation for the quest for Native American spirituality, often undertaken with the greatest sincerity, actually comes from the ego, sentimentality, or the self-defeating desire for some otherworldly experience. Non-Natives who try to conduct their "own" ceremonies, such as a Plains Indian sweat lodge, may not fully comprehend the ceremonies' place within a unified lifeway. Under such conditions, there is no guarantee that what is found will not lead to further frustration and thus to an intensification of the original problem.

Additional problems arise when non-Natives make an attempt to "become Indian." This impulse represents a new form of colonialism in America: now that we have taken over the land and resources, we want to acquire the nonmaterial culture as well. Often, non-Natives attempt this by cobbling together traditions from various tribes and other world religions to form what they believe is an authentic spiritual path. This denies the reality that Native American ceremonies emerge from very specific worldviews; they are not interchangeable. Ceremonies lose clarity, for example, when Navajo chantway songs and Buddhist meditation are incorporated into a Plains pipe ceremony. Some non-Natives believe they can purchase access to Native spirituality by attending occasional weekend retreats. Sometimes these retreats are run by non-Natives who have not undergone the years of extensive training recognized by the tribes in question. Nonetheless, these "white shamans" sell the right to participate in Native ceremonies. Yet Native American spirituality cannot be bought with a credit card. For those Native Americans who follow traditions, these traditions infuse every moment of every day.

Very often when I speak about the relevance and the reality of Native American values, I am misunderstood by students who like to believe that I am encouraging them to "become Indian." This is not my point at all. One has to be brought up in these cultures and live the languages in order to truly identify with the ethos of a Native American people. What non-Natives can do, however, is use these traditions as models that provide answers to some of the problems we are facing in our own society.

Native American cultures present a model of what a religious tradition *is*, and this is a basic reality of which we have lost sight. What really is a true religious tradition? What does it encompass, what are its dimensions? Native American cultures demonstrate how all components of a culture can be interconnected, how the presence of the sacred can permeate all lifeways to such a degree that what we call religion is here integrated into the totality of life and into all of life's activities. Religion here is so pervasive in life that there is probably no Native American language in which there is a term that could be translated as "religion" in the way we understand it. As Peter Nabokov tells us in his book, *Indian Running*, when you track down a seemingly isolated or minimal feature of Indian life, such as running, the whole system opens before your eyes—and this is true because of the interrelatedness of all the components of a genuine tradition.[1] Obviously, in such a system life cannot be fragmented, because of that binding and interconnecting thread of the presence of the sacred.

Once non-Natives come to see what an authentic religious tradition is, they can revitalize those same components in their own traditions. The model provided by Native American traditions can help people recover some of the unraveled threads of their proper history, heritage, and sacred realities. With the few selected examples I offer in my work, I aspire to give a brief sampling of some of the core Native American values and perspectives. Through these, non-Natives can perhaps come to relearn a little bit about themselves and about their own proper spiritual heritage, with the hope that what has been lost can still be rediscovered. Certainly, the Native American people themselves, especially the younger ones today, are trying to regain and to revitalize their own traditions that may have been lost or taken from them through a variety of pressures and prejudices. Non-Natives have in this struggle, I suggest, a model for their own proper quests.

It is a perilous undertaking and a heavy responsibility to presume to speak of the sacred traditions of another people. I have attempted in my teaching and writing to find an approach that does not violate the integrity of the cultures discussed. I often refer to the ideal potential built into Native traditions but do not mean to promote some idealized view of Native American cultures. The potential inherent in these traditions may or may not be realized depending on specific families, tribes, reservations, and political and economic constraints. I also recognize that there are several hundred tribal groups spreading over numerous geographical areas and representing at least a dozen mutually unintelligible language families that encompass hundreds of dialects. I suggest, however, that, in spite of this enormous diversity, it is possible to identify shared core or root themes that seem to undergird the traditions of all these groups, even though they are expressed through a rich variety of means. It is these shared themes that provide a structure for much of my work: time, sacred place, language and oral transmission, art, the metaphysics of nature, and the transformative power of ritual.

These categories of religious experience may make sense to the non-Native, but most Native Americans experience them as a whole. While non-Natives may deduce and formulate theologies for the people, in their experience there are no theological structures that stand alone and independent of experience and realization. We thus do not find the kinds of differentiations, separations, and dichotomies familiar to Western culture. Religion and life are here one, and that is why, in non-Native languages, there are no terms for "religion," just as there is no term for "art." All in life and thought is interrelated like a vast spider's web, a form often referred to in Native American myths, tales, and art forms.

It is important that approaches to Native American religious traditions be rigorous and scholarly in the best Western sense. But, in addition to such reification of the subject, it is also essential that we come to understand these traditions, so far as is possible, as they are lived by *human individuals*. Native American traditions should be understood as Native Americans themselves experience them. One way we can do this is to turn to the vital, living traditions of today, as well as to the stories of long ago. Many Americans assume these traditions are relics of the past that have gone the way of the open plains and the buffalo. Yet Native American lifeways did not become extinct. They have changed, adapted, and been sustained despite numerous campaigns aimed at their destruction. As Margaret Vickers (Tsimshian-Kwa Gulth) has commented, "There's so much talk about the 'rebirth' of our cultural heritage. That's another misconception. It has never left us. People speak of our pride and our dignity in the past tense. We've always had it. And we always will, as long as we respect ourselves and other living beings."[2] Getting a glimpse of how Native American religious traditions are lived today offers us a deeper understanding of their meaning and significance than does relying on past stereotypes and assumptions.

In order to know who we are, it is essential to have some means of comparison, whether across other civilizations, cultures, lifeways, and languages, or the possibility of relating to, and contrasting oneself with, nonhuman beings. Native Americans can learn more about themselves by learning about other tribes. The same is true for non-Natives. We can hope that a true and open dialogue will emerge from the dual search of Native Americans and non-Natives in which neither attempts to imitate the other but through which both may ultimately regain and enrich the sacred dimensions of their own respective traditions.

Southwestern Pueblo people often objectify the realities and dynamics of experience through the *kachinas*, sometimes called "gods." There is an account of a Zuni kachina who emerged from the underworld attached back to back with a white man. Back to back, it was suggested, the Zuni and the white man will have to struggle to see and understand each other. The fact remains, however, that the two are attached. If there is any hope, it lies in the possibility that there may come a time for a turning around so that they may know who they are in relation to the other and what they both might become.

TWO

Changeless at the Heart of Change

Concepts of Time and Process

CONCEPTS OF TIME and process are central to a people's worldview and generate a particular quality of life and culture. Non-Native, Western culture, for instance, often perceives time as a linear progression that advances from past to present to future in a straight line. According to this understanding, humans evolve and progress along the increments of the time line. In contrast, many Native American cultures observe that the rhythm of the world is circular, as is the life of all beings and forms. In these cultures, time tends to be experienced as cyclical and rhythmic, rather than linear and progress oriented. Most Native American languages, for instance, do not have past and future tenses; they reflect instead a perennial reality of the present.

These differing perceptions of time have contributed to the misunderstandings that characterize so many interactions between Native and non-Native Americans. A culture organized around the number of seconds and minutes ticking by has difficulty comprehending a culture patterned after natural occurrences such as moon cycles, animal migrations, and tidal changes. Carl Sweezy, an Arapaho painter born in 1881, elaborates on some of these differences:

> White people who did not try so hard to understand the ways of the Cheyenne and the Arapaho as we did to understand their ways, thought we were all lazy. That was because we took a

different attitude toward time from theirs. We enjoyed time; they measured it. . . . We had no set time for coming back [from a hunt], for that depended on the buffalo and on the weather. When we had meat enough and the skins were dry enough to pack, we started back to the home camp.[1]

The different perspectives are further complicated today now that digital clocks and time cards have been incorporated into reservation life. Conflicts can arise for Native Americans between seasonal ceremonial calendars and daily work schedules. Nonetheless, many Native American traditions continue to be oriented toward cyclical time, despite the influences of mainstream culture. Because these contrasting concepts of time persist, we can gain some clarification of our personal and social tensions by coming to understand the nature and the implications of linear and cyclical time.

Linear versus Cyclical Time

The concept of linear time has deep roots in Western society. It first emerged in certain Judaic perspectives and became fully entrenched during the European Renaissance and the Age of Enlightenment. Although Western culture recognizes the cycles of days, calendar years, and agricultural seasons, there is an overarching sense that time is forever marching forward out of the past and into the future in a straight line. The concept of time as a straight line has come to permeate many aspects of Western life. Not only do Western languages revolve around past, present, and future tenses, but common sayings encourage people to "line up!" or "let's get this straight!" When someone is not making sense, people might say he or she is "talking in circles," or they might make circular motions alongside their head to indicate that the person is a little crazy. Dominant American culture has even laid this preference for straight lines onto the natural landscape. City planners follow the lines of the grid, while the U.S. Army Corps of Engineers tries to straighten the course of waterways such as the great Columbia River.

Linear time and process is not just a neutral, quantitative scale of measurement but is inseparable from the values that give rise to it in the first place. For instance, linear time has generated the myth of

Interior of Navajo Hogan. Photo by Jonathan Wilson.

progress. This myth claims that things are getting better all the time, that Western culture knows more now than it ever has, and that life will only improve in the future. Of course, there are ups and downs along the way, but culture is inevitably marching forward. The belief includes an assumption that everything that came earlier on the time line is somehow inferior to the more recent. For years, this assumption permeated the way scholars viewed Native American traditions. Since Native American societies were considered a remnant of the primitive past, they were thought to occupy a low rung on the ladder of civilization, while modern American culture was quickly climbing to the top. Such views provided justification for the injustices perpetuated against Native Americans and their natural environment. They helped fuel, for instance, the frenzy of "Manifest Destiny," in which settlers believed they should spread their notion of progress from sea to shining sea. The residues of this belief still plague us today.

A core perspective and an accompanying human problem in linear time is the reality that the straight line of time does not support the experience of a center. The linear form suggests movement from or toward indefinite ends, thus denying the human person the possibility of relating to a center of permanence. Such a center gives significance to change, for change is meaningless unless it is in relation to the changeless. Without a return to the center, the experience of time can seem fragmented. For instance, people oriented toward both past and future are likely to be distracted from the human and spiritual possibilities inherent in being in the *now*.

In contrast to linear concepts of time, most Native American traditions follow the example of nature and perceive that cyclical, not linear, processes of change are inherent in all forms and patterns of nature, such as the life cycles of animals, the ebb and flow of water, the growth of plants, the turning of the seasons. In traditional Native cultures, humans experience time by interacting with these natural cycles and by orchestrating their actions to fit the cycles' rhythms. Time, then, is based not on abstract measurements of sixty seconds or twenty-four hours but on the processes that sustain life. For instance, Florence Kennedy, an Inupiat woman, spent her early years hunting and fishing for subsistence along the Bering Sea. In her late fifties, she moved to Seattle, where the instant gratification of consumerism makes her nervous. She explains: "Up there in the bush, I was more patient. In the deer season, you knew when the deer were going to come down from the high places. You knew when the fish were leaving the streams or coming back. You knew when the berries were ripe. You learned to wait for the night to be over. You learned to wait through a time of hunger, to wait for an old person to die."[2] In this type of environment, humans do not force processes to comply with their timetables. Rather, they respect the cycles of other beings and of life itself. And they learn to wait and observe.

Because these cyclical patterns continue to revolve, there is always an opportunity for life cycles to be renewed. Unlike linear time, which marches straight into the future, cyclical time loops around and starts again and again. Winter leads to another spring, the death of a deer leads to the continued life of a human family, a harvest renders more seeds for planting. While these events certainly occur regardless of differing worldviews, modern Western society does not often focus on or honor them. Countless Native American rituals, however, draw strength and rejuvenation from cyclical return. Each year, for instance, the Iroquois celebrate planting and harvesting ceremonies for their maple syrup, strawberry, squash, bean, and corn crops. In the dead of winter, they gather for the Midwinter ceremony in which they ask the Creator that all things continue in the new year as they have in the past. Old fires are extinguished and new fires are kindled, cures are strengthened, and old power dreams are renewed. In essence, the world of the Iroquois begins again for another annual cycle. Through such re-creating activities, change is recognized and honored, but at the same time it is explicitly affirmed in its relationship to the changeless, which is the center of every circle or cycle.

Many tribes believe that these renewal ceremonies, far from being mere New Year's celebrations, are responsible for sustaining life. The Pueblos of the Southwest follow a very strict ceremonial calendar during which humans impersonate, and thus become, sacred beings. This periodic return of the deities reestablishes contact with the realm of the sacred. Without the seasonal enactment of these rites and ceremonies, tribal members believe that the recycling of the sacred world- and life-sustaining powers will cease, the world will die, and the people will be no more. In a similar way, a central goal of the annual Plains Sun Dance is the regeneration or renewal not only of the individual dancers but also of the tribe and, ultimately, of the entire universe. The Sun Dance honors the source of all life so that the world and humankind may continue in the cycles of giving, receiving, bearing, being born, growing, becoming, returning to the earth, and, finally, being born again.

In addition to ceremonies that renew annual cycles, many Native cultures also mark the cycles of human life. Many tribes hold that as the human life moves from birth to death, it recapitulates the cycles of the cosmos, the sun, and the seasons. Just as these cosmic cycles embody continuity and renewal, so, too, does the process of human life, for when this process is understood in a cyclical rather than in a linear manner, death inevitably returns to or joins life so that the cycle may continue. We can see an extension of this belief in hunting cultures, in which humans assumed the sacred responsibility for taking the life of living beings and so became partners, or links, in the cyclical chain of life and death—they believed that there would be life again. The implications of such beliefs to spiritually meaningful concepts of death are of the greatest importance and offer alternatives to the linear understanding of death as "the end of the line."

This cyclical reality was beautifully expressed in a living manner for me when I noticed how the dignified old Lakota man Black

Elk would relate to little children. He would get down on his hands and knees and pretend he was a horse, and the children would squeal with joy on the old man's back. There obviously was no generation gap; he fully connected with the children. I once asked him how it was that he could so relate to the children, and he replied: "I who am an old man am about to return *to* the Great Mysterious and a young child is a being who has just come *from* the Great Mysterious; so it is that we are very close together." Because of this cyclical understanding, both are almost at the same point.

Time in this context is experienced as a seamless unity. Stages of life fold into the present, for, in the cycle of time/life, what we have experienced becomes integrated into who we are now. This process fosters expansion and wholeness, rather than the contraction and fragmentation so typical of linear perspective, in which what one has passed through is progressively left behind. Orientation toward unity, in which the cycles of human life are in sync with cosmic patterns, fosters a quality of life that is rich in potential. Esther Nahgahnub, an elder from the Fond Du Lac Ojibwa reservation in northern Minnesota, reminds us of the type of life that can grow out of cyclical time:

> Long ago when white people came to our villages, it looked to them as if we only worked when we wanted to, which was in essence true. You didn't have to hunt unless you wanted to eat, or needed something to put on when winter was coming on. But we had time for the necessary things; the development of the mind and heart; we had the time to be contemplative. We had the time to see the relationship of all things to each other.[3]

Amid the busy schedules and overextension of modern Western society, many people "run out of the time" it takes to stop and perceive the relationship of all things. Wedded as it is to a sense of time separated from nature, Western culture does not offer much time to cultivate relationships with our families, our surroundings, the beings with whom we share the land. In contrast, Esther Nahgahub's words remind us that living in the present allows us to be in immediate and continual interrelationship with the qualities and forces of our natural environment.

Just as the cycles of nature rotate and return, the time of myth is continually reexperienced within Native American traditions. Mythic time refers to the period when the world was created, when figures like Coyote and Raven roamed the earth shaping ridges, cutting coulees, bestowing plants and animals with characteristics, teaching ceremonies, and even creating human beings. It is a time of trans- formation and fluid distinctions. Many tribes, for instance, say that in the mythic time, beings had the ability to change shape, from animal to human and back again. It is also a time when land, beings, and rituals were given spiritual power. The Navajo explain that it is in the long ago that First Man and First Woman breathed life into the four sacred mountains that define Navajoland. The Salish of the Northwest speak of the mythic time when the Great Spirit turned his wife into the ribbed, conical shape of the sweat lodge, making her one of the most powerful spirits that humans can encounter.

In the Western understanding of linear time, all of these mythic events would be a relic of the distant past. Yet, since many Native cultures perceive time as cyclical, they hold that mythic time has the potential to fold into the present moment. For instance, the Great Spirit's wife did not enter into *one* specific Salish sweat lodge on *one* occasion in the past. Rather, she is continually present in the sweat lodge, always infusing it with her power. Similarly, when a Navajo family builds a *hogan*—a traditional house that is held up by four posts—not only do they follow the same pattern First Woman and First Man used for forming the four sacred mountains, but they also participate in the same mythic process of creation. In other words, the world's beginnings are recapitulated in the actions of daily life. The past is a separate but touching layer that lies beneath everyday existence. It is as if the present world were of a transparent nature through which mythology can penetrate at any time.

While the cycles of mythic time revolve with their own force, humans can cultivate a connection with mythic time through certain ceremonies and actions. People encourage the return of mythic time, because it is a time of great spiritual power, a time when the process of creation is ever-present and rituals are performed in their original, most potent form. One of the ways in which people draw upon mythic power is by reciting the myths themselves. Most Native American cultures stress that myths are not stories created by humans but truths revealed by suprahuman powers. To remind listeners that reciting a myth is a sacred, powerful process, some storytellers preface the myths with special phrases. The Lakota artist Arthur Amiotte says that when a Lakota storyteller uses the phrase *Mitakuyepi*, which means "my relatives" or "my everything," the audience knows that something profound is about to be said.[4] Next, the storyteller might use the phrase *Ehanni*, dragging out the pronunciation to *Ehaaaaaaaaaaaanni*, which is the equivalent of saying "long, long, long ago." This "long ago," it should now be clear, does not refer to a historical period of a linear time past but usually refers to a qualitative condition of existence. By telling the myth, that quality may be mysteriously reintegrated into the present.

Words themselves are thought to have the power to reintegrate myth into today. While there is a tremendous diversity among Native American oral traditions, most tribes believe that language has creative force. Words are not merely symbols that point to things; they call forth the reality and power of the being mentioned. To name a being in these languages is to actually make it present. The Koyukon of Alaska, for example, do not refer to the bear by its proper name, for to do so would make the power of the bear present and most likely offend this potentially dangerous animal. To avoid this, a Koyukon man looking for a bear den might say, "Wait, I see something: I am looking everywhere for a lost arrow."[5] His companions would know that one looks for a bear den in the same way one looks for arrows.

Because words have this kind of power, telling myths is a sacred act that imposes serious responsibilities upon the speaker. Calling forth the presence of mythic beings cannot be done carelessly. The Chippewa-Cree will not tell myths involving the Thunder Beings until the Thunder Beings have safely traveled south after the last fall storm, for they are far too powerful to draw into in one's living room. Similarly, the Navajo wait to tell certain stories about bears and spiders until these animals, who have negative capabilities, have gone underground in the winter.

Because of the generative power inherent in most Native languages, the telling of myths has the ability to make mythic time present, a part of the now. This seeming contradiction of the past becoming present is captured in the customs of Zuni story telling.

When Zuni people recount myths, they are not supposed to mention any modern developments such as cars or electricity; they must restrict their story to the long ago. At the same time, they must impersonate characters and use hand gestures to make it seem as though the myth is taking place now, in the present, right in front of the audience. The story has to be a part of the long ago, yet still be a part of present moment. The power of oral transmission makes this possible. Zuni storytellers do not merely refer to a myth of the past; they call it forth with the power of the spoken word.

In addition to reciting myths, performing ceremonies can also recreate mythic time. During rituals, participants may enter into a sense of timelessness, or time outside of ordinary time. In the Apache girls' puberty rite, for instance, just as a ceremonial tipi is constructed to create sacred space, special songs are also sung at the beginning and the end of the ceremony to delineate the sacred time of ritual. The repetition of songs, drum rhythms, and prayers heightens the feeling that time is suspended during the ceremony. It is as if no time has passed between the first song and the last song, or between the present ceremony and the one first performed for the deity *Isdzanadl'esh*, or Changing Woman, in mythic time. Repeating a myth in this atmosphere intensifies the sense that the girls are actually participating in the original experience, rather than listening to a story about the past.

Some rituals require that people reenact mythic events. By carefully imitating the gestures and words of mythic figures, they rejoin those figures at the creation of the world. For example, the Yurok of Northern California believe that, in the beginning, the world was inhabited by the *wo'gey*, or Immortals, who knew how to live in harmony with the earth. The *wo'gey* departed when the humans arrived. Yet, because they knew that humans did not always follow the laws of the world, they taught them how to perform ceremonies that could restore the earth's balance. Now, when the Yurok perform the Jump Dance every two years, they carefully repeat the speeches and actions the *wo'gey* dictated to them in mythic time. Through this process of ritual imitation, they become the *wo'gey*. They, too, have the power to return the world to its original state of beauty and harmony. Rather than bring people back into mythic time, this ritual brings the mythic time of creation into the present. In this context, creation is not a thing of the past, but an ongoing process. When the Yurok perform their dances, they renew the world for today.

Mythic time surfaces not only in ritual ceremonies; it also pervades daily life. Many of the shapes and forms of the natural landscape are embodiments of mythic events. Salish people, for instance, tell the story of how Coyote and Fox passed through the Bitterroot Valley in western Montana preparing the world for humans. Down in the southern tip of the valley, Coyote got into a fight with Big Horn Sheep. Coyote made Big Horn Sheep so angry that the ram charged after him. Tricky Coyote, however, stepped out of the way, and the ram crashed right into the trunk of a ponderosa pine. That happened in the long ago, but Big Horn Sheep's horns are still lodged in the tree. Today, the Salish drive from miles around to pray and leave tobacco offerings at the tree, because they know that special power still resides there.

Mythic time also makes itself present in interactions between humans and animals. When the Koyukon hunt in the subarctic forests of Alaska, sometimes they come upon a caribou killed by a wolf but hardly eaten. The Koyukon know that in the Distant Time, when animals and humans used to speak the same language, wolves and people hunted together and shared their kill. Now, although wolves and humans have separated into different societies, it is believed that wolves still feel that mythic connection. From time to time, they leave their kill for humans, and, in return, traditional Koyukon people do not mind if wolves sometimes help themselves to parts of the animals they have hunted. While a non-Koyukon person might overlook the significance of this human-and-wolf interaction, Koyukon tradition encourages people to notice how myth is continually coming to the surface. People live in the present moment, knowing that the present is intimately connected with the mythic past.

*Creation Stories: The Algonquin Earth Diver
and the Zuni Emergence*

The Cheyenne say they emerged into this world from a dark, underground cave. The Nez Perce say they were created from the blood of the Monster that Coyote killed near Kamiah, Idaho. While the specific stories vary, every tribe has a creation myth that describes the making of the world and the origin of human beings. Scientists and historians often dispute the factual basis of these creation stories. They claim that, instead of originating in North America, tribes migrated to this continent from Asia over the Bering Land Bridge. In contrast, most creation stories assert that the indigenous tribes came into being on their native soil. The author Vi Hilbert, a member of the Upper Skagit tribe of Washington, says,

> When I lecture, I discount the Bering Land Bridge theory—our legends give us proof that we've always been here. We know where the first mountains came from, we know where the mother came down from the sky world, pregnant with her child. She gave birth, and this is what created the Sun and Moon. It is our epic story of creation. It takes one hour to tell. It's my way of telling the powers that be that we've always been here.[6]

Part of this conflict in perspective stems from the difference between scientific and mythic truth. Most tribal creation stories focus not on how tribes got to a certain place but on how the tribes became who they are. The stories explain a tribe's relationship to the land, other beings, and the Creator. They shape ritual ceremonies. And, as part of mythic time, they continue to recur each time they are told. While they may not offer a scientist's version of empirical fact, they do embody profound truth that gives meaning to tribal traditions. There are hundreds of myths that embody these truths, but, unfortunately, I can discuss only a few here.

Although some non-Natives view Native American creation stories as simplistic and unrealistic, in reality, they reflect a highly complex conception of the universe. Many Southwestern creation myths, for instance, envision the cosmos as a number of spheres pierced through by a hollow vertical axis. The Zuni believe there are seven spheres, with the top sphere being the realm of *A'wonawil'ona*, the supreme life-giving, bisexual power. Other spheres are identified with the Sun Father, who gives light and warmth, and the Moon Mother, who gives light at night, divides the year into months, and expresses the life cycle of living beings. The fourth sphere is the terrestrial realm, which is associated with the Earth Mother, the provider of all vegetation.

Before the Zuni emerged into the terrestrial realm, they inhabited a dark underworld where the Sun Father did not shine. People jostled and stepped on each other in the pitch black, and cries of anguish filled the air. Sun Father decided it was time to bring the people into His presence. He created two sons with supernatural power and instructed them to lead the people out of the underworld. The sons descended into the darkness and told the people to follow them. They tossed a line of corn meal into the air to light the way. Then the sons planted a ponderosa pine tree, which the people used to climb into the third world. Once in the third world, the people climbed a spruce tree into the second world and then a quaking aspen into the first world. Finally, they scaled a silver spruce and emerged into this world, where the Sun Father shone brightly down on them. As the people moved through the emergence process, they learned how to make pray sticks and sing sacred songs. They also came to respect the sacred power of the trees and animals that helped them along the way. These lessons learned in mythic time continue to shape Zuni religious traditions today.

The Tewa, the Zuni's Pueblo neighbors, envision an equally sophisticated yet different emergence process. The Tewa also began in a dark underworld, yet, instead of being cramped and uncomfortable, this was a fluid and sacred realm in which humans, animals, and supernaturals lived together and death did not exist. Although the supernaturals stayed below, the humans ascended into this world, where death and evil were present. Before the emergence of humans, the Tewa describe the world as *ochu*, meaning green, unripe, and eminently sacred. After humans' emergence, the world becomes *seh t'a*, or dry, hardened, and ripe.

Thus, the Tewa emergence trajectory moves from the sacred world below to the more profane world of today—comparatively a realm of hardness, limit, and restricted possibility. This duality is reflected in much of Tewa tradition and social organization. Tewa people, for instance, are divided into two groups: the Summer people and the Winter people. This social structure reflects the Tewa belief that the universe consists of two complementary parts, which cannot be separated from each other. As the creation myth illustrates, it is from this duality that life comes forth.

Far from the dry lands of the Southwestern Pueblo, the Algonquin peoples of the Eastern Woodlands and the Plains tell of how the world was formed in the midst of a vast body of water. There are many versions to this creation myth. The Blackfeet, for instance, say that, in the beginning, there was water everywhere. *Napi* (Old Man) and all the animals rested on an old raft floating across the water. *Napi* wanted to make land, so he told the beaver to dive into the water and bring up some mud. The beaver jumped into the water, and, although he stayed under a long time, he could not reach the bottom. So the loon tried instead, and the otter after him, but the water was just too deep for them. At last the muskrat was sent down for the fourth try. He was gone a long time—so long the animals thought he must have drowned. But at last he surfaced and bobbed on the water, almost dead. When they pulled him up on the raft and looked in his paws, they found mud clenched inside them. *Napi* dried the mud and scattered it over the water, forming the land.

There are many variations on this Earth-Diver myth that follow a similar pattern. Some say the Earth Maker sent a different variety of animals down into the water. The southern Ontario Ojibwa say the earth was brought up on the back of a turtle. In this account, the turtle represents, or is, the earth, as well as fertility. Through the agency of breath, Earth Maker then fashions and enlarges the earth, establishing its features and contours until it is again a suitable habitation for all the beings of water and land, finally including human beings.

The key themes in these accounts illustrate a message of immediacy. The creation of land where there is only water takes place not out of nothingness but within the perspective of cyclical progress, for land was there before this particular deluge and thus is now underneath the waters and must be recovered. Further, Napi of the Blackfeet or the Great Hare among the central Algonquins is already there upon these waters; in some versions he is holding the people's most sacred pipe, often identified with creation and creative power. Indeed, all the aquatic birds and animals are already created and present with Earth Maker. Their presence shifts the orientation away from creation understood as a single event of time past to the reality of those immediately experienced processes of creation that are ever occurring and recurring in cyclical fashion, just as the observable cycle of days or seasons speak of death and rebirth.

This reality of the continuing creative process, experienced in the manifestation of the sacred in the present and witnessed through every form and force of nature, offers the outsider a key to understanding the cycles of time in Native American religious traditions.

THREE

Fixing a Center

Native American Sacred Geography

IF ALTERNATIVES ARE being sought today to linear, progress-laden concepts of time, there is also the parallel quest for a new understanding and appreciation of place. Many people are interested in learning about Native American interactions with the land, because these cultures have been rooted in the American landscape for thousands of years. Indeed, Native American affirmations of the interrelated sacredness of time and place are spelled out across our land with enormous creative diversity. Yet, despite their great variety and their thousands of distinct sacred sites, Native American cultures share some fundamental principles in their relationships with the land.

Unfortunately, Native American connections to the land have been subject to overromanticization. Some non-Natives cherish the stereotype of Natives Americans communing with nature in a "pure," emotional manner. Far from being sentimental, however, Native American relationships with the land are often deeply embedded in the heart of Native traditions. "To us when your land is gone, you are walking towards a slow spiritual death. We have come to the point that death is better than living without your spirituality," says Carrie Dann, who along with her sister Mary has led a twenty-year legal battle to gain access to Shoshone land in Nevada.[1] More and more, people realize that this type of deep commitment to the land is essential to all people. At a recent development conference in Arizona, executives from a coal company tried to persuade Navajo tribal leaders that the economic benefits of coal mining would keep the tribe alive. An elderly Navajo woman stood up and replied, "With our prayers and our sings, we keep you alive."

Many tribes believe in the sustaining power of the land. Indeed, according to most Native American traditions, land is alive. Every particular form of the land is experienced as the locus of qualitatively different spirit beings. Their presence sanctifies and gives meaning to the land in all its details and contours. These spirits also give meaning to the lives of people who cannot conceive of themselves apart from the land. The recognition of a multitude of spirits does not preclude all of these spirits from coming together in one unitary principle. Like the spokes of a wheel, the spirits meet at the center in what some tribes refer to as the Great Mysterious or the Creator.

While all land is alive, mythic events can layer certain places with additional spiritual significance. The Kiowa author N. Scott Momaday explains how mythic time and sacred place converge: "Time has a spatial extension, that which once happened literally took place, and still has a place."[2] Mythic events can thus be experienced repeatedly through landmarks in each people's immediate natural environment. For instance, the waterfall where Coyote got into trouble or the place where a tribe emerged into this world continues to embody the power of mythic time. People return to these sites to pray, to fast, or to gather special herbs, for they know the places have the power to respond to their requests.

Native American groups maintain the presiding sense of the sacred that is present in their land by entering into relationship with the land. These relationships constitute a sacred reciprocity. "Nobody owns the land," explains Virginia Poole, a Seminole/Miccosukee from the Everglades. "We said we'd watch over it, because that's our responsibility. You just take care of the land, and it takes care of you."[3] The land nurtures the people by sharing its power, giving songs for ceremonies, herbs for healing, and visions for strength. In turn, people honor the land by treating it with respect, performing ceremonies, and singing songs of thanks.

Today, however, it is difficult for some tribes to conduct the appropriate rituals, since many sacred sites are on private property

Navajo boy riding. Photo by Jonathan Wilson.

or managed by government agencies. The Bitterroot Salish, for instance, were forcibly removed from their homeland in Montana's Bitterroot Valley to a reservation a hundred miles north. Now, when the Salish archeologist Marcia Pablo Cross travels to the sacred sites in the valley, she says she can feel that the places are lonely. She says it is as if they are whispering, "Where are you? Why haven't you been doing your dances?"[4] When elders are able to pray at the sites, the mountains, the river, and the creeks seem to soak up the words. Those prayers of thanks are necessary to maintain a balanced relationship between the land and the people. When they go unspoken, the land becomes lonely, and the people who live in the valley today remain removed from the power that surrounds them.

Such an awareness of the sacred power of nature, immediately experienced rather than dangerously abstracted, speaks with particular force to the root causes of many of today's problems, especially to our present ecological crisis. It is perhaps this message of the sacred nature of the land, of place, that has been most responsible for bringing Native American traditions to the mind and conscience of the non-Native American.

Because the land contains spiritual power, many tribes look to the land for assistance and guidance. In the rocky arroyos and the fresh water springs of Southern Arizona, for instance, the White Mountain Apache see reminders of how to live a good Apache life. For them, the land is not only alive; it is a moral force. It holds within it deposits of an ethical code that shows the Apache how to act in a just manner. Wilson Lavender, an Apache from Cibecue, Arizona, describes the role the land plays in his life: "One time I went to L.A., training for mechanic. It was no good, sure no good. I start drinking, hang around bars all the time. I start getting into trouble with my wife, fight sometimes with her. It was bad. I forget about this country here around Cibecue. I forget all the names and stories. I don't hear them in my mind anymore. I forget how to live right, forget how to be strong."[5]

The names and the stories Lavender mentions are the tools the Apache use to access and interpret the moral power of the land. The Apache landscape is densely populated with places that have specific names. Mountains, ridges, springs, creek beds, and rocks are given sentence-long, vividly descriptive names such as 'water flows downward on top of a series of flat rocks' or, 'white rocks lie above in a compact cluster.' The descriptions are so evocative that the place quickly becomes present in the mind of the listener. The Apache take great pleasure in using place names in their everyday speech. The anthropologist Keith Basso recalls a time when he was stringing a barbed-wire fence with two Apache cowboys from Cibecue. One of the cowboys started talking quietly to himself, and, when Basso leaned closer to hear, he realized the cowboy was reciting place names. Later, when Basso asked him about it, he said he liked to do that because, "I ride that way in my mind."

All of these place names have stories connected with them. Indeed, these stories constitute a specific genre, referred to as historical tales, within Apache oral tradition. Historical tales recount events that occurred in specific places in Apache territory, usually before the coming of the white man, though some focus on the reservation era. They tell of the troubles that befall people who transgress Apache norms. By detailing the ruptures of society, they outline appropriate behavior. The Apache elder Nick Thompson explains that his-

26

torical tales are used to prod people into living appropriately: "We shoot each other with them, like arrows." When a person is not acting in accordance with Apache custom, Thompson says, "someone goes hunting for you . . . someone stalks you and tells a story about what happened long ago." The tales take only about five minutes to tell, for, like the arrows they are meant to resemble, they work best when they move quickly.

Unlike any other form of myth or story, historical tales open and close with the speaking of the place name where the tale occurred. If the person who is shot with a historical tale changes his or her behavior, the Apache believe that person will have a lasting bond with the place described in the tale. Thompson explains:

> You won't forget that story. You're going to see the place where it happened, maybe every day if it's near-by and close to Cibecue. If you don't see it, you're going to hear its name and see it in your mind. It doesn't matter if you get old—that place will keep on stalking you like the one who shot you with the story. Maybe that person will die. Even so, that place will keep on stalking you. It's like that person is alive.

During his work among the Western Apache, Basso saw how the historical tales work in action. In the summer of 1977, a seventeen-year-old Apache woman came to observe a girls' puberty ceremony with pink plastic curlers in her hair. While this type of attire was considered fashionable at the young woman's Utah boarding school, Apache women are expected to wear their hair loose at puberty ceremonials. This practice is important, since the ritual is effective only when all the participants follow the prescribed customs of respect. Though no one spoke directly to the young woman in curlers, she was the object of quiet disapproval.

A few weeks later, Basso saw the young woman at a small party at her grandmother's house. In the midst of casual conversation, the grandmother, told a version of the following story:

> *ndee dah naazííh yú 'ágodzaa.* (It happened at 'men stand above here and there.')
> Long ago, a man killed a cow off the reservation. The cow belonged to a whiteman. The man was arrested by a police-

man living at Cibecue at *ndee dah naazííh yú 'ágodzaa* ('men stand above here and there'). The policeman was an Apache. The policeman took the man to the head Army officer at Fort Apache. There, at Fort Apache, the head Army officer questioned him. "What do you want?" he said. The policeman said, "I need cartridges and food." The policeman said nothing about the man who had killed the whiteman's cow. That night some people spoke to the policeman. "It is best to report on him," they said to him. The next day the policeman returned to the head Army officer. "Now what do you want?" he said. The policeman said, "Yesterday I was going to say 'hello' and 'good-bye' but I forgot to do it." Again he said nothing about the man he arrested. Someone was working with words on his mind. The policeman returned with the man to Cibecue. He released him at *ndee dah naazííh yú 'ágodzaa* ('men stand above here and there').

ndee dah naazííh yú 'ágodzaa. (It happened at 'men stand above here and there.')

To the Western Apache listeners at the party, this story was an explicit indictment of people who try to behave like the white man. While it was acceptable for the Apache man to kill a cow during the poverty of early reservation years, it was not acceptable for another Apache to turn him in. Because he has transgressed this custom, the policeman falls under the spell of witchcraft, which made him appear forgetful and foolish. A short time after the grandmother told this story, the young woman stood up and left the party. Basso asked if there was something wrong, to which the grandmother responded, "No. I shot her with an arrow." In other words, she had aimed the historical tale at the granddaughter.

Basso ran into the same young woman a few years later. When he asked if she remembered that incident, she recalled that when she realized her grandmother's story was meant for her, she grew embarrassed and ashamed. She threw her curlers away. As they drove toward the young woman's camp, they passed close to *ndee dah naaziih* ('men stand above here and there'), the spot where her grandmother's story took place. When Basso pointed the place out to the young woman, she said nothing at first. Then she answered quietly in Apache, "I know that place. It stalks me every day."

After a relative or friend has told an historical tale, the place itself becomes the moral force that draws people back onto the Apache path. Benson Lewis of Cibecue explains, "I think of that mountain called 'white rocks lies above in a compact cluster' as if it were my maternal grandmother. I recall stories of how it once was at that mountain." The storyteller will die, but the events of the story are fused into the land, becoming a constant reminder of what it means to live a good life. In this way, the land nurtures the Western Apache. "The land is always stalking people. The land makes people live right. The land looks after us," says the Western Apache woman Annie Peaches. When people stumble, the land is there to catch them. When some one forgets, says Nick Thompson, the names of the places "make you remember how to live right, so you want to re-place yourself again." Because of the land's role in their lives, the Apache know that they are surrounded by benevolence. "These are all good places," says Nick Thompson. "Goodness is all around."

When Time Takes Place: The Navajo Landscape

Like their Apache neighbors, the Navajo have a relationship with the land that is shaped by oral tradition. The telling of myths provide the Navajo with a map to the power and significance of their surrounding landscape. The myths detail events that occurred in mythic time, such as the birth of Changing Woman, who created the Navajo from her skin, or the slaying of the monsters to make the world safe. These events did not occur in an ethereal netherworld, however. They took place at specific geographical locations in the traditional Navajo homeland in what are now the states of Arizona, New Mexico, Colorado, and Utah. When these mythic times touched down on the earth, they infused the land with power.

Walking through Navajoland is a constant reminder of mythic reality. Star Mountain, for instance, still bears within it the power it received from a mythic event. In the long ago, before the Navajo people were created, Monster Slayer and Born For Water were responsible for killing all the monsters who inhabited the earth. As the boys pursued one of the monsters, Talking Rock, over the top of a mountain, they hit him and chipped off a piece of his body. The chip was shiny, like a star or a crystal, and it landed on the ridge of the mountain, and so the mountain became known as Star Mountain. The piece of Traveling Rock remained on Star Mountain until traders or missionaries took the crystal away in the nineteenth century. Although the crystal has disappeared, the Navajo know the place has special power because of the mythic events that transpired there. To this day, medicine men journey to Star Mountain to perform ceremonies and to collect small crystals believed to be splinters from Traveling Rock itself.[6]

When all the monsters were killed, the Sun persuaded Changing Woman to move to the west. She left her home at Huerfano Mountain (in present-day New Mexico) and traveled across the Navajo homeland. Along the way, Changing Woman stopped in many places, giving each her power. For instance, she rested at a set of falls in the Little Colorado River. Since then, the falls have been a good place to offer prayers, for the power of the place can carry those prayers to the Creator. At another spot on her journey west, Changing Woman stopped to have lunch. After eating, she stuck her planting stick into the ground and created a spring, while the crumbs of her blue corn bread turned into a large round rock. Today, people go to this place to offer prayers for basic necessities such as food and water.[7]

The tradition of stopping to pray at these sacred sites helps make the mythic time present. According to the Navajo, the journey of Changing Woman is not an event that occurred once in the distant past, in the way that Jesus Christ was born at one specific time in Christian history. Instead, because her journey is etched on the land, it is continually reoccurring. The crumbs from her lunch are always present; the power she placed in the land still responds to human prayers. In her movement from the east to the west, Changing Woman follows the pattern of the sun from dawn to dusk, the current of the San Juan and Colorado Rivers from the mountains to the Pacific Ocean.[8] Just as these natural cycles are always unfolding, Changing Woman is continually entering into the land.

Events that set these mythic cycles in motion are not limited to "the long ago." In 1863, for instance, while Kit Carson was leading a United States Army campaign to intern the Navajo at Fort Sumner, a small group of Navajo fled to the western edge of Navajoland. In the distance, they saw the Head of Earth Woman (Navajo Mountain), a mountain shaped like a loaf of blue cornbread. They slipped behind it, and, as the army closed in, a miraculous event took place.

Monster Slayer, the hero who had cleared the earth of monsters in mythic time, was suddenly reborn on top of the Head of Earth Woman. Like a rain cloud in the monsoon season, he was born and raised in the course of one day. Clothed in a suit of flint armor, he and the Head of Earth Woman formed a shield between the Navajo and Kit Carson's army. The army was repelled, and the band was one of the few that escaped the Navajo's four years of confinement and starvation at Fort Sumner. This is but one of many mythic events that has transpired in more recent times. For the Navajo, the land always has the potential to become a stage for the actions of the Holy People, a vessel for their power.

Just as the land hosts these mythic events, it also generates ceremonies for the Navajo people. Monster Slayer's appearance on the Head of Earth Woman inspired the Protectionway, a ceremony performed to ask for protection, to avoid misfortune, or to pray for something to happen in one day. During the ceremony, an invisible shield of armor is invoked by prayer and held over the patient's head to shelter the person from destructive forces. Like most Navajo ceremonies, the Protectionway draws power from the land. Patients pray directly to the Head of Earth Woman:

> Head of Earth, on the top!
> Head of Earth, by your holy power may I also be holy power.
> With this power I will be spared.
> With this power with which you talk may I talk.[9]

Such ceremonies are part of a reciprocal relationship in which the land shares its power with the Navajo and the Navajo offer their thanks and respect by performing the ceremonies and retelling the myths.

While mythic events give significance to certain places, it must be stressed that the entire Navajo landscape is thought to be sacred by the people. The landscape is not a surface of patchwork sites physically and spiritually isolated from one another. All created forms of the landscape have a spiritual essence. All are alive. In their 1994 study of Navajo sacred places, Klara Bonsack Kelley and Harris Francis write that, while there are qualitative differences between places, Navajo elders believe that no one place is more "sacred" than another.[10] There is a unity, a series of relationships that binds all places together.

This unity can be fractured when pieces of it are destroyed. The strip mining and dam projects that plague Navajoland not only damage the spirits of the particular places but also endanger the overall fabric of Navajo tradition. The Head of Earth Woman, for instance, is connected to the power at nearby Rainbow Bridge. If the Head of Earth Woman were to be mined, both the Protectionway and the ceremonies that draw on Rainbow Bridge would suffer. Some Navajo believe that they do not have the right to make decisions about developing the land, for it does not belong to human beings. Mamie Salt, a Navajo elder, says, "This is Changing Woman's land, only she can say, 'It's my land.' Only hell is everybody's land."[11] According to Mamie Salt, hell is a land that has no spirits to claim it.

The Battle for Sacred Lands: The Sweet Grass Hills

When Native American tribes bring these types of sacred land struggles to the courts and media, they often confront mainstream America's inability to understand the concept of sacred land. With its roots in agrarian society, American culture typically perceives land as something to be utilized or manipulated. For instance, when a group of business people looks at the Sweet Grass Hills in North Central Montana, they see an opportunity to make money by leaching gold from mountain ore. In contrast, the numerous Plains tribes see the Sweet Grass Hills as a part of an intricate web that connects the people to the Creator, the elements, the animal beings, the plant beings, and tribal ceremonies. Mining in the Sweet Grass Hills would disrupt the entire web. "It's like when you make medicine to cure some one," says the Chippewa-Cree tribal member Don Good Voice. "If you are missing one ingredient, it won't work. That's how it is with the Sweet Grass Hills. Our medicine, ceremonies, prayers— without the Hills, none of it will be as effective."[12]

The three conical buttes of the Sweet Grass Hills are visible for more than a hundred miles as they rise 3,000 feet above the prairie floor. Just as they define the horizon in this flat country, they have shaped the traditions of the Chippewa-Cree, Blackfeet, Mandan, Arikara, Assiniboine, Gros Ventre, Salish, Kootenai, and Northern Cheyenne and their ancestors for millennia.[13] Some tribes believe the Hills are part of a constellation of sacred sites that includes Chief

Sweet Grass Hills, North Central Montana. Photo by Marina Weatherly.

Mountain in the Rocky Mountains, the Medicine Wheel in Wyoming, and the Black Hills in South Dakota. Many of the tribes that use the Sweet Grass Hills were traditional enemies, but the Hills were a neutral zone in which no one could be attacked. As long as people carried no weapons on their journey to the Hills, tribes knew that visitors had come to pray. People went alone to fast for visions or gathered together for ceremonies. Aerial photographs of the Sweet Grass Hills reveal two to three thousands tipi rings etched by centuries of Sun Dance ceremonies.

What draws so many Native people to the Sweet Grass Hills is their sacred power. Like the Navajo, many Plains tribes recognize that, while all land is sacred, certain places have qualitatively distinct sacred power. The Hills are not simply preferred hunting grounds or a good place for summer encampments; they are the locus of mythic events. For instance, the Chippewa-Cree believe that the Hills are where the Creator began remaking the world after the great flood. They also say that, when the buffalo were annihilated in the nineteenth century, they descended into a large cave in the Hill's West Butte, a belief underscored by the fact that the Hills were one of the last areas where buffalo were found before their demise.[14]

The Sweetgrass Hills also play a role in Blackfeet mythology. When a young Blackfeet man named Scarface set out to talk to Creator Sun, he went first to the Sweet Grass Hills to fast for the knowledge necessary to find the Creator. On the last night of the young Blackfeet's fast, the spirit of the East Butte came to him, infused him with its power, and told him where he had to go next. Scarface's fast in the Hills launched a journey that culminated in meeting the Creator Sun and returning home with instructions on how to perform the ceremony that became known as the Sun Dance.

Contemporary stories continue to tell of powerful events that occur in the Sweet Grass Hills. Don Good Voice tells of a Chippewa-Cree man who went to the Hills to fast. On his way there, he stopped to ask a rancher which access road he should take to the West Butte. After the rancher gave the man directions, he asked, "So, are you going up there to fast? When you get up there, could you ask those spirits to come down and give me some rain for my crops?" The man agreed and headed into the West Butte. On his fast, he prayed for the rancher, and, as he did, rain came and drenched the fields. Don Good Voice ends this story by saying, "To me that is like a small example of the power of those mountains. You ask for something as simple as water, as simple as rain, and you get it. Just think what we could ask if we were serious as human beings going there to ask for peace, to turn world events around."

It is because of this power that the Hills have become embedded in Chippewa-Cree and other religious traditions. Don Good Voice explains, "Since time immemorial, the Sweet Grass Hills was one of the focal points of our tribe to seek out spiritual guidance, a spiritual sense of belonging." People journey to the Hills to fast and to communicate with the Creator. Fasting for a vision is a physically and spiritually exacting ceremony. Individuals go without food or water for four days and expose themselves to the elements and the spirits. Chippewa-Cree elders say that when people fasted in the old days, they accepted the possibility that they would die in the process. The Sweet Grass Hills repay that sacrifice by giving the people spiritual power. They endow people with the strength to heal illnesses or face life's challenges. They give the people more than 350 plants for medicinal and ceremonial use. Perhaps most important, the Hills give songs the Chippewa-Cree use in their ceremonies, songs that allow them to communicate with the spirits. The tribal elder Pat Chief Stick stresses, "Those songs are not composed."[15] Rather, they are given by the spirits in the Hills.

The Chippewa-Cree's relationship with the Sweet Grass Hills is a part of the larger sense of relatedness the tribe maintains with the world around it. Pat Chief Stick explains: "Here's what the old people tell us. The mountains, the air, the water, the wind, the rock, the wood, everything in the ecology—we use every bit of the ecology in our religious ceremonies. These things, wind, air, mountains, water, rock, Indian religion, are connected. Whenever we do the ceremonies, we gather all that stuff. That's the reason why they're so powerful." And if one of those elements is destroyed, the ceremonies and the tradition could suffer. All the tribes that have prayed in the Sweet Grass Hills are now facing the possibility that a powerful tie to their tradition may be severed because of open pit gold mining. This process involves stripping the ore from the mountain side and drenching it with a cyanide solution to separate the gold from the ore. The cyanide contaminates the water, while the crushed ore releases poisonous metals such as lead, mercury, and arsenic. With 80 percent of gold mined today used for jewelry, the consequences of this type of destruction reveal startling priorities.

When they realized the potential devastation that was threatening the Hills, seven tribal governments launched a protest campaign. Unfortunately, however, the tribes face a difficult challenge. Although the federal government has prohibited mining on public lands in the Hills, it claims that it cannot stop mining on private lands. Most court cases related to religious freedom refer to practices, such as a Jewish soldier's wearing a yarmulke in the army or an Amish child's going to a public school. The courts fail to recognize that sacred land is essential to Native American religious practices and that, when the natural state of sacred land is disturbed, the whole tradition suffers. A National Register of Historic Places report on the Sweetgrass Hills makes that crucial connection: "Native American cultural leaders teach that this spiritual presence is not necessarily a permanent condition, but can only exist with the context of an undisturbed natural setting. Substantial disruption of the natural pristine qualities of the Sweetgrass Hills will displease the spirit life and spirit powers, and may cause them to leave forever."[16] Protecting a few vision spots while mining the rest of the Hills does little to solve the problem, since the spirits of the land are interconnected. "These Hills are not just sacred in one place. Every bit of those mountains are sacred," Pat Chief Stick says simply.

With a temporary moratorium on mining in the Sweet Grass Hills, the tribes continue to find legal and legislative ways to stop future mining. In the meantime, many also turn to prayer. Don Good Voice says that at an annual intertribal camp in the Sweet Grass Hills, people pray "that owners of the mines will change their minds and see that these mountains are just as alive as anybody and that they want to live too. We pray that they will respect that sanctity of life and the spirituality of those Hills."

At the Center of the Universe: Sacred Architecture

The sense of place that roots a tribe in the earth is not only located in the land. It is also generated in the process of building homes and ceremonial structures. The tipi, the earthlodge, or the longhouse— like the temple, the cathedral, or the sacred city center of antiquity— determines the perimeters of space in a way that establishes a sacred center. This center is an axis between heaven and earth, an axis that pierces through a multiplicity of worlds. Living at the center, then, orients humans to the place where all things meet.

The myths that infuse the landscape with power also give meaning to architectural structures, since many of the myths that explain the creation of the world also describe the creation of buildings. According to Navajo creation myth, for instance, constructing a hogan is a reenactment of the mythic time when First Man and First Woman created the four sacred mountains that delineate the Navajo homeland. Navajo place the four supporting poles in the four directions, just like First Man and First Woman placed the sacred mountains in the east, west, north, and south. As Roberta Blackgoat, a Navajo elder who is resisting a government-imposed relocation from her homeland, explains, the four sacred mountains "are all part of the room inside our hogan . . . the Creator set these mountains down for our hogan posts."[17] Living in such structures places daily life at the center of mythic patterns.

For many tribes, the sacred center is movable. The nomadic tribes of the Plains, for instance, establish their center wherever they place their tipis. Each of these shelters represents the universe. The circular edge defines the bounds of the universe, and the open fire in the center is the presence of the Great Mysterious—the center of all existence. Traditionally, each member of the family has a special place to sit around the tipi's frame, a practice that defines an individual's identity in relation to the sacred, central fire. The smoke hole at the top of the tipi allows smoke to carry prayers to the spirits, while the poles form a funnel that draws down power from above. Thus, the tipi's structure creates an exchange between this world and the heavens.

Like the rituals that connect people to sacred places, many traditional forms of architecture have ceremonies that accompany their construction. These rituals help place the inhabitants in relation to the center. When a new tipi is first pitched, for instance, a holy person is often asked to pray to the Great Mysterious for blessings on the home and its inhabitants. When the Lakota construct their sweat lodges, they carefully align the willow frame in accordance with the four cardinal directions, with the door facing east, from where the light of wisdom comes. To build the central altar, they place a stick at the center of the lodge and draw a circle around it, offering the following prayer: "By fixing this center in the earth, I remember You to whom my body will return, but above all I think of *Wakan-Tanka*, with whom our spirits become as one."[18] Without such ritual fixing of a center, there can be no circumference, and with neither center nor circumference a person cannot know where he or she stands.

A ritually defined center is not just a mathematically fixed point established arbitrarily in space. It is also taken to be the actual center of the world. The Pueblo people of the Southwest believe the center of the world is the spot where they emerged from the underworld into this one. They refer to this place as the *sipapu*, or earth navel. Around the *sipapu*, the people build a round, adobe structure called a kiva, in which they perform ceremonies related to the world's creation. What often challenges non-Native understanding is the fact that every pueblo has a *sipapu*, and some pueblos have more than one. This means there are multiple centers of the world. Within the reality of myth and cyclical time, this is perfectly logical, for the emergence is an ongoing event that recurs through the ritual process. Each time a particular ceremony occurs in a kiva, that *sipapu* becomes the place of emergence.

Just as the Pueblo emergence process is etched on the springs, caves, and mountains of the Southwest, it is also carved into Pueblo

Blackfeet Tipi. Photographer unknown. Photo No. 79-65. Collection, K. Ross Toole Archives, University of Montana, used by permission.

kivas. Some Pueblo tribes say they began in the first world, a most sacred lower world in which animals, humans, and spirits could communicate with one another. Slowly humans emerged through a series of worlds until they came to this one, the fourth world. The structure of the kiva reflects this scheme. On the floor of the kiva is a deep hole representing the *sipapu*, the access to the sacred lower world. The space within the kiva represents the second world, while the bench running along the walls is the third world. The ladder pointing out of the small, circular opening leads to the fourth world and then continues into the sky and the worlds of the heavens. As people descend into and rise out of the kiva during ceremonies, they retrace the steps of the original emergence.

Many Native American structures reflect an image not only of the universe but also of the human being. As such, they remind their inhabitants that, like the kiva or the hogan, they, too, bear the sacred center within themselves. The Plains Sun Dance lodge, for example, is a temporary structure, built out of saplings and brush, that creates a space for dancing, prayer, curing, and sacrifice. At the heart of the lodge stands the center pole, a sacred cottonwood tree,

Crow women setting up tipi at Crow Fair, Montana. Photographer unknown.

rooted in the earth and stretching up to the heavens. Over a three- or four-day period, dancers move from the circular edge of the lodge to the tree at the center and back again, always facing and concentrating upon the center pole. The Lakota artist and writer Arthur Amiotte explains that dancing in this manner within the lodge helps "men to realize that there is a sacred world whose center is everywhere, including inside himself; and that our whole life is journey towards it."[19] Such structures and places found within our American land may serve as reminders to those who have lost or forgotten the sense of a center.

FOUR

Silence, the Word, and the Sacred

Evoking the Sacred through Language and Song

Songs are thoughts, sung out with the breath when people are moved by great forces and ordinary speech no longer suffices. Man is moved just like the ice floe sailing here and there in the current. His thoughts are driven by a flowing force when he feels joy, when he feels fear, when he feels sorrow. Thoughts can wash over him like a flood, making his breath come in gasps and his heart throb. Something, like an abatement in the weather, will keep him thawed up. And then it will happen that we, who always think we are small, will feel still smaller. And we will fear to use words. But it will happen that the words we need will come of themselves. When the words we want to use shoot up of themselves, we get a new song.

—Orpingalik, Netsilik shaman

WITH THESE WORDS, Orpingalik, a Netsilik Eskimo shaman, eloquently expresses the power, mystery, and inspiration of language and song. This rich legacy is carried within all the still surviving Native American languages. Through ignorance or ill will, however, this legacy has been largely ignored or purposely destroyed by a dominant English- or French speaking majority. This situation may be called tragic, not because of some vague romanticism, but rather because it impoverishes non-Natives, who are therefore not aware of the remarkable range of sacred values imbedded in such languages. A major contributor in the progressive compromising of tribal lan-

guages is the prejudicial assumption of the Western world that literacy is an unqualified good and an indispensable prerequisite for culture. The persistence of this prejudice against nonliterate communication has contributed, perhaps more than any other element, not just to the compromise of most indigenous cultures of America but, in numerous cases, to their actual extinction, since ultimately it is language that bears culture.

Western society would do well to look back in time to Plato's dialogues in the *Phaedrus*, where Socrates tells us of the god Theuth, who came to Thamus, the King of upper Egypt, telling him that writing "is a branch of learning that will make the people of Egypt wiser and improve their memories; my discovery provides a recipe for memory and wisdom." To this the King replied,

> If men learn this, it will implant forgetfulness in their souls.
> They will cease to exercise memory because they rely on that which is written, calling things to remembrance no longer from within themselves, but by means of external marks. What you have discovered is a recipe not of memory, but for reminder. And it is no true wisdom that you offer your disciples, but only its semblance, for by telling them of many things without teaching them, you will make them seem to know much, and as men filled not with wisdom, but with the conceit of wisdom, they will be a burden to their fellows. . . . Anyone who supposes that such writing will provide something reliable and permanent, must be exceedingly simple-minded.

At the heart of Native American and Inuit cultures, we find to this day living expressions similar to this Greek wisdom and even elements that go beyond the understandings of the Classical world. Among all Native American and Inuit languages, for example, there is a blending of rich verbal and nonverbal expressions. In this mode of communication, the processes of life and time are experienced in a cyclical manner, not in the linear view that characterizes Western literacy.

Further, in Native American languages, the spoken word or name bears an immediate sacred presence. Words are produced through the agency of breath, and in these traditions, the breath, whether human or nonhuman, is understood as a physical expression of the sacred life principle. The source of breath is the lungs, which reside next to the heart, often understood to be the spiritual essence or center of the living being. It is because of this understanding that, among hunting peoples, when an animal or sea mammal is slain, the hunter blows his breath into the nostrils of the slain being as a ritual act of responsibility by which the taken life breath is restored.

Extension of this sacred understanding of breath and the spoken word is provided by Robert Williamson in his important 1974 study, *Eskimo Underground*:

> *Sila* is the word for air, without air there is no life; air is in all people and all creatures; anything deprived of air ceases to live. In that air therefore gives life and without air there is no life, that Eskimos believed that they are part of the Life-Giving Spirit, that each individual is animated by the Life-Giving Spirit, and that they are part of his soul, that part which is the essence of all things living, is part of the ultimate deity of *Sila*. . . . This is of course something which never dies, air and the life-giving force go on indefinitely, so then does the soul of men. When the air passes out of the body at the moment of physical death, it is simply passing out of the soul back into its original matrix.[1]

Closely associated with these Inuit realities is the people's understanding that spoken names or words are not understood symbolically or dualistically, as they are in English. In Native languages, to name or speak of a person, a being, or some phenomenon in Nature is to make present or call forth the spiritual essence of that which is named. In this regard, Williamson, through his Arctic research, tells us further that

> The Eskimo believed that the emitting of a word evoked an image, which was an actual reality. No one could say that an image once invoked, by being spoken, was not a reality, though a mental one. The language is a complex of mental images, but not the physical objects, and the words used to evoke them are, in Eskimo thinking, equally real. The name of an individual is more than a label, it is the name whereby a person's separate social existence is evoked, it is the symbolization of

his personality, it is his very essence, and the spiritual and functional means whereby he is identified and related with the rest of his society and his physical and metaphysical environment.[2]

The spoken or audible word, then, is experienced by Native Americans in a manner very distinct from Western modes. To the Western mind, at least outside specific liturgical contexts, the spoken word is conceived as symbol. The relationship between the spoken sound and its meaning is based on a somewhat arbitrary consensus. Such separation of experience is not possible in Native American languages, in which a mysterious identity between sound and meaning exists. To name a being, or any aspect or function of creation, actualizes that reality.

For example, if one were to speak the Lakota words *Wanble Galeshka*, or Spotted Eagle, one would experience an immediate contact with the specific powers of that most revered being. In this context, words and names are understood not as metaphors but as conveyors of spiritual realities. Given this sacred nature of language, it is virtually impossible to engage in verbal profanities. When I was living with Black Elk's family on the Pine Ridge Reservation in South Dakota, I remember a time when an old man was repairing the roof above us. He was singing a Lakota song as he worked, when all of a sudden, we heard in loud English, "God damn it!" Apparently, he had hit his thumb with the hammer. I soon came to the understanding that for a Lakota to use profanity, it was necessary to branch out into English.

Since naming a being makes manifest the power or quality of that which is named, personal names tend to be used carefully in Native American languages. One avoids using one's own or another person's sacred name and, especially, out of both respect and awe, the name of a deceased person. As the Kiowa author N. Scott Momaday writes in his autobiography, *The Names*: "A man's life proceeds from his name, in the way that a river proceeds from its source."[3] Names are chosen with great care, for, as Momaday observes, it is through one's name that one's identity is achieved; people become their names. The Lakota leaders Carole Anne Heart and Arvol Looking Horse spent a year choosing the right name for their daughter, because, Carole Anne explains, "We wanted to give her one that would carry her throughout her entire life. . . . It's like saying to a child, 'You're going to be a high-achieving woman. You're going to live up to your name.'"[4] Some people choose to change their name when things are not going well for them, for a new name can give a life a new direction.

Because names carry such power, they are reserved most often for prayer and ceremonies. For other occasions, the Lakota, as well as other tribes, use kinship terms to establish a relationship between speakers. Instead of using an elder woman's name, the Lakota might say "Grandmother." These generational terms correspond directly to sacred realities beyond the human family. For example, the Lakota term for 'Grandfather,' *Tunkashila*, means "the Great Spirit" or "the Creator." *Unchi*, or 'Grandmother,' means "the Earth" or "the Bearer of Life." These terms, carried by the breath, a being's most sacred element, connect people not only with each other but also with great spiritual powers.

As these examples demonstrate, words do not merely describe; they create. The Navajo believe that, while the Holy People thought the world into being, those thoughts were not actualized until words were uttered in prayer. Speech for the Navajo is associated with action, with the transformation of substance, the molding of air and breath.[5] The spoken word can, therefore, shape reality. This is why in almost every Navajo ceremony, the phrase *Sa'ah Naagháii Bik'eh Hózhó* is repeated several times, for those words call forth beauty, harmony, and long life. Conversely, there are certain words associated with war that Navajo warriors are allowed to use only within the context of battle. To speak 'war talk' at any other time would induce the enemy to attack.[6]

As I came to learn through my own experience, the Lakota have a similar understanding of the creative power of the word. When I lived with Black Elk and his family, Black Elk shared with me a hunting song that could call in the animals. He told me that I must never overuse it but sing it only when times were very hard. That winter, game was especially scarce, and the family was becoming desperately hungry. I hunted for days without seeing any sign of deer. Finally, I sat on a bluff, and, with no game in sight, I began singing Black Elk's song. After several minutes of singing, a herd of deer appeared.

Words have this generative power especially when they are spoken in a world of unified experience. Native American cultures per-

Navajo drummer. Photo by Jonathan Wilson.

ceive the bonds that join all humans, animals, natural forces, and landscape together. Because of the continual relationship and communication between beings, animal spirits and spirits of the land respond to the spoken words of humans, and, if they are fortunate, human beings can learn to understand the language of other beings. A. I. Hallowell, for example, recounts a conversation an Ojibwe couple overheard:

[T]here was one clap of thunder after another. Suddenly the old man turned to his wife and asked, "Did you hear what was said?" "No," she replied, "I didn't catch it." The old man thought that one of the Thunder Birds had said something to him. He was reacting to this sound in the same way as he would respond to a human being, whose words he did not understand. The casualness of the remark and even the trivial character of the anecdote demonstrate the psychological depth of the "social relations" with other than human beings.[7]

In Western culture, however, dichotomies separate humans from direct communication with other beings. In European languages, spoken words, along with animals and the natural world, are often seen as objects. While words on a page can certainly influence people, they do not carry the power within themselves to communicate with the larger environment or generate reality.

Cultures that recognize the power of the word realize how carefully words must be used. Speech is a manifestation of power, and speaking is a sacred act that imposes serious responsibilities upon the speaker. As the Kiowa writer N. Scott Momaday says, "If I do not speak with care, my words are wasted. If I do not listen with care, words are lost. If I do not remember carefully, the very purpose of words is frustrated. This respect for words suggests an inherent morality in man's understanding and use of language."[8] Similarly, the Crow word for 'talk' is translated in English as "breaking with the mouth." It is understood that once a word has left the mouth, it has consequence in the world. Examples of how this sense of responsibility permeates life are numerous. For instance, the Makah Cultural and Research Center in Washington State records oral histories, but, unlike other tribal archives, the tapes are not available to the general public, researchers, or even other tribal members unless the contributing elder offers explicit permission. Ann Renker, a member of the Makah Nation, explains, "Our elders are not afraid of death. What they are afraid of is having their words and their things used wrong later on."[9]

For many Native American cultures, words are not the only mode of communication, for silence itself constitutes language. In Western culture, we often fear silence. We are so uncomfortable with it that we fill it up with all kinds of insignificant noise and words. We do not let the power inherent in silence communicate with us. Cultures based on oral transmission, however, recognize that without silence, there cannot be language. They recognize that in silence there are profound modes of sacred, humanizing communication. As Black Elk said, "Silence is the voice of the Great Mysterious."

The Value of Oral Transmission

The sacred power of the word infuses the oral traditions of non-literate societies with deeply positive values. I use the term nonliterate rather than illiterate, since the latter connotes the inability to read and write, an inability that is considered negative and derogatory. Too often, we have branded people as backward and uncivilized if they are illiterate, whereas one can make a strong case for the advantages of growing up and living in a nonliterate society. In such a society knowledge is borne *within* the individual in a living manner; you do not have to go outside of yourself, for all that is essential to life is carried within you. Native American cultures have adopted the written word, as evidenced in the upsurge of contemporary fiction and nonfiction written by Native Americans. However, many traditional values, relationships, and experiences are best expressed through oral transmission in the Native language.

Providentially, memory and oral transmission of traditional Native American myths, folktales, law, and stories are a living reality today. The continuation of traditions by the means of Native languages constitutes a powerful response to those dehumanizing contemporary modes of interpersonal communication such as the computer languages of technology or television. Even our excessive and obsessive fix on the written word, for all its practical advantages, is possessed at great cost, of which we have become tragically unaware. While I realize that literacy has its positive elements and is absolutely essential to conditions of contemporary life, I think we should consider what has been taken away from us as a result. For example, the act of reading itself conditions us to lineality. This is something we do not often think of as we read a book, back and forth, back and forth. Through this process, we participate in a lineal perspective that, among other things, can contribute to the loss of those circular, reciprocal perspectives that reinforce a host of ultimate values within nonliterate traditions.

In such oral traditions, preserved within the individual being, the process of transmission necessarily involves personal, interactive dimensions of communication that reach beyond the spoken word and certainly beyond the written word. These transmissions are carried by the breath, or for trees and grass by the breath of the wind, and this breath proceeds from the inner area of the heart. When it is released, it is shared with all that it touches. Everything in creation—animals, birds, mountains, trees, rocks, and rivers—communicates its specific powers to those who are able or who have been taught to listen. It is in such understanding that there lies a quality of language that may be called sacred.

It is only through such intensely personal encounters that there becomes possible a quality of understanding that simply cannot be acquired through any amount of "book learning." This fact explains, I believe, the great difficulties many Native Americans experience in their attempt to participate in those educational structures of the non-Native world that rely so much on worksheets and multiple-choice tests. There is a kind of tragedy in this situation, for Native Americans, certainly, but also for the non-Indians' educational structures, which would stand to gain immensely if they could incorporate certain aspects of the Native Americans' philosophy of education. The quest of so many students today to relate more experientially to the school or university curriculum is evidence of this deeply rooted need for the personal encounter.

The fact, therefore, that so many Native Americans are redesigning their own educational systems, structured for their own needs, should be seen as a positive, new direction. It is especially heartening since countless Native Americans were forced to attend—often against their parents' wishes—Draconian government boarding schools. These schools recognized that much of a people's worldview can be communicated only in that people's own language, and so they forbade students to speak Native languages. The experience of a Crow woman, Susie Yellowtail, in the 1930s, was frightfully common:

> They would wash our mouths out real good with homemade grease and lye soap whenever they caught us talking Crow. I loved speaking Crow so much and would keep talking it anyway. I remember once I was severely punished for speaking Crow. They made me kneel on a broomstick for several hours in a corner on the floor of the laundry. I passed out several times. Each time, they picked me up and put me right back on that hard broomstick. It was terrible.[10]

So effective was this brutal indoctrination that when Susie Yellowtail returned to the Crow reservation, she had to be pressured by her relatives to speak Crow again. She later became a tireless spokeswoman for Native American education and tribally run schools. It is in light of this type of experience that the new emphasis on regaining command of Native languages and creating Native language curricula is so significant. Across the country, tribal schools have launched Native American bilingual programs for children and adults. Where Native languages are being thus sustained, oral traditions are communicating core values to all members of the tribe.

The Keepers of the Oral Traditions: The Elders

Most Native American societies store oral tradition within the elders of the community, giving the elders of the society a special role and quality of being. Like the speaking of the word, the telling of myths and stories actually recreates the event. The power generated by the re-creation becomes integrated into the person speaking the words. The elder becomes the medium for the message of the myths. It is as if, in part, he or she is made alive by the word. Such a person cannot fail to command respect by fulfilling a function of infinite value to the society. The Acoma poet Simon Ortiz recalls listening to the older men of the Pueblo talking as they repaired the adobe on the village walls: . . . "the men who keep up the traditions of our people, community, of our language. These are the people who insure that the language keeps being a way of *touching* among ourselves, the things we see and hear, the things that we all are enjoined with, those things around *all* of us."[11]

Universally in these societies, elders serve as models of ethical behavior. Their age and accumulated knowledge are woven into wisdom in an experiential process of learning through life. Life is seen as a successive integration of the stages of child, youth, middle age, and old age through which a person becomes whole. This view of a being's totality may be contrasted with our own segmentation of life, which often assigns elders to a position on the margins of society. Given the fragmentation of the modern family, the place of elders in this culture is all too often in the nursing home, where they frequently feel lonely, isolated, and without purpose in the larger society.

In most Native American cultures, however, elders are fully linked to the life of the tribe through their role as transmitters. They have the very significant task of passing on knowledge to the young people. The following account, given by the Lakota Charles Alexander Eastman (*Oheyesa*) in the nineteenth century, still resonates today:

> The distinctive work of both grandparents is that of acquaint-ing the youth with the [peoples'] traditions and beliefs. It is reserved for them to repeat the time-hallowed tales with dig-nity and authority, so as to lead him into his inheritance in the stored-up wisdom and experience of the race. The old are dedicated to the service of the young, as their teachers and advisers, and the young in turn regard them with love and reverence.[12]

Often, when elders tell the young people a story, they show children respect by not providing too much didactic analysis. To do so is thought to be wrong, for it would rob the child of his or her own true learning experience through direct observation.

By passing on oral traditions, the elders keep young and the young grow into maturity of age. This is an eminently humanizing process. The Crow woman Susie Yellowtail's memories of being looked after by a famous Crow leader, Chief Plenty Coups, illustrate the tender-ness and respect elders and children can share:

Crow elder Susie Yellowtail visiting with grandchild. Photo by Michael Abramson.

Chief Plenty Coups would baby-sit the children while the grown-ups were having their fun. He was a really wonderful man. What I remember most about him was his kindness and love for children. He never had any children of his own, but was always caring for someone else's children. He was crippled then and a wise old boy. He used to take us outside at night and all the children would pile up on his lap and sprawl out under a big old tree. He'd point out the stars and tell us long stories way into the night. The story about the Big Dipper took three or four nights. Was that a telling! He would also tell war stories about his adventures during raids in the old days. Everyone loved him.[13]

When I was a young boy growing up in Maine, I used to go down to the shore, where I would find Abenaki and Penobscot elders telling stories about the area where my family lived. Those stories brought to life elements of that world that I had not been aware of in the academic environment. Not only is this type of teaching and learning alive and well in Native American homes and families throughout the country, but it is also now being brought into the schools. On and off reservations, elders are being asked to come into the classroom to tell stories to the children, often in their own Native languages. Lawrence Aripa, a Coeur d'Alene elder from Idaho, frequently accepts invitations to speak in schools, because, he says, "the stories were handed to my grandfather and now I hand them to the children. The stories are our textbooks; they teach and our children need these stories."[14] As an educator, it seems to me there is no more effective mode of communication and education than through such person-to-person oral transmissions.

Since oral tradition speaks even to the youngest in the group, it creates bridges of understanding between the generations. Oral tradition can thus be addressed with special force to the problems of generational segmentation and individual alienation so typical of much of the American world today. It is my suggestion that in Western culture, there are traditions somewhat parallel to these Native American attitudes, but they have been lost in the emphasis on the nuclear family, in which the elders are often placed in nonfamilial guardianship outside the mainstream of family and society. Western society's fear of death has resulted in the deceptive efforts of the elderly to stay "young at heart," rather than accept the dignity concomitant with being an elder and the sanctity that comes with understanding death. It is possible to stem the tide of this segregation by rediscovering with originality Western culture's own traditions. Social problems need the immediate attention of welfare and housing programs, but, ultimately, we will need to rekindle the deeper cultural forces that grant honor and respect to the total person.

"Make It Like It's Right in Front of You":
The Art of Storytelling

As Kah-ge-ga-gah-bowh (George Copway), a member of the Ojibwa tribe, wrote in 1858, "There is not a lake or mountain that has not connected with it some story of delight and wonder, and nearly every beast and bird is the subject of some story-teller."[15] The same is true today, when a drive past a certain knoll, an outing to pick bitterroots, or a request from a grandchild are the type of daily events that draw forth stories, myths, and tales. The elders who most often tell these stories are great artists; they are actors who are able to tell stories in a way that quickly catches the attention of the children, the old people, everyone. Such speakers bring the event to life so that listeners of all ages are taken into the event in an immediate manner. The subject of the recitation—whether it is a Trickster Coyote tale or a creation myth—is not an event in lineal time past but is of the immediate moment, as real now as it ever was or will be.

Oral transmission bears culture not only because it conveys the lore of Native American traditions but also because it embodies one of their most sacred values: relationship. Storytelling is a communal act; there must be a speaker and at least one listener. With a book, both the writer and the reader have a solitary experience from which they can disengage at any time. With oral transmission, however, listeners must participate in a story with the teller. Often, the language of stories is spare and terse, for so active is the role of the listeners that they are expected to fill in the descriptive details of appearance and setting with their own imagination.[16] Many storytellers will speak only as long as their audience utters words of encouragement or makes hand gestures that demonstrate that they are still in the story. Crow woman Susie Yellowtail recalls how she kept the storytellers talking:

> When I was a little girl, every so often in the evening my family would invite some old man into our home. We would make cherry pudding for him and have him tell stories to us kids. As long as we said, "Eh," which is "yes," he kept on telling the story. When nobody said "Eh" that was the end of the story. He'd quit and go home. Then he'd come back and do it again another time. Most often, I'd be the last one going "Eh" and everybody else would be asleep. I'd just love those stories. That was the way we told stories in those days.[17]

While books are objects that focus on what happened, stories are events that are in the process of becoming. People can enjoy the same Coyote story over and over again, because each telling, setting, context, audience, each moment turns it into something different. As Dennis Tedlock has said,

> An oral story is not an object of art or any other kind of object. It is an action, it is something I do. It's an action that's now, and that speaks of ancient things. If we get into storing that in a book we've begun to forget. We begin to attribute the past

to that book which if we please we can put up on the shelf and forget. A book that was published in 1789, that was published in 1801, that was published in 1902. Those are like tombstones. The story is what I'm telling now with my own breath. With my own body.[18]

Stories are living events that draw their significance from the people who participate in them. The Laguna writer Leslie Marmon Silko explains, "Writing down a story, even tape-recording stories, doesn't save them in the sense of saving their life within a community. Stories stay alive within the community like the Laguna Pueblo community because the stories have a life of their own. . . . The old folks at Laguna would say, 'If it's important, you'll remember it.'"[19]

"If you're really true to a story," a Zuni storyteller told Dennis Tedlock, "you make it like it's right in front of you."[20] Great storytellers employ a multitude of rhetorical devices to convey this type of immediacy. They may use the first person, and the present rather than the past tense, thus telling the account as if they are really present, even actually engaged in dialogue with the figures of the narrative. Storytellers pay attention to precise detail, making events in the narrative occur at specific geographical sites well known in the immediate environment of the listeners. They use their voices artfully to convey the sounds of the animals of the narration, while the lengthening of vowels in adjectives and verbs conveys the sense of duration or distance. The intensity of voice is adjusted to fit the particular action being described, or silence may be used to heighten tension or suspense or may indicate that the narrator is engaged in personal prayer. They skillfully manipulate language and delivery to fit the character in question. Often, they use rich metaphor as well as metonymy (using a part for a whole). The beaver, for example, may be referred to among the western Shoshone as "bigtail owner," which offers insight into the beaver's traits. Ritual enactments often accompany the mythic account, as well as props, hand gestures, and mnemonic devices such as the birch bark scrolls of the Ojibwa. Songs specific to a sacred being of the account may be interjected, or even a personal sacred song of the narrator.

In addition to the special nature of the Native American languages themselves, the recounting of a myth is made special through the insistence that the telling of the account is serious and potentially dangerous, so that there must be both an appropriate time and place for such telling. Coyote stories, for instance, may not be told after the first thunder in spring or before the last thunder in the fall, when the Thunder-Beings are around. Severe punishments may befall the speaker if he or she does not follow storytelling prescriptions carefully. The Kiowa believe that if they tell a story about their Trickster figure during the day, he will bite their noses off. The Santee Sioux warn that when the wrong story is being told in the summer a snake might slither right into the house and wrap itself around the storyteller. These restrictions strengthen the sense of immediacy, for they demonstrate that the power of what is being said is so great that it can influence the workings of the world.

There is a great sense of immediacy in the telling of myth, since many tribes view myth not as a lifeless narrative form but as a vital entity with the power to create the world. To recite in the particular tribal language a myth dealing with creation is actually to make present in the here and now those sacred events of a mythical time. For instance, the Ojibwa word for myth, *atíso'kanak*, is the same as the words for "our grandfathers." Often the grandfathers will visit when their stories are being told, making their presence felt during the telling.

Myths have the power to explain the world. Yet, as Rodney Frey has pointed out, this trait often leads to misunderstanding. To reduce myth to this one function suggests that there is a separation between the story and the reality; in other words, "myths account for the world." For most Native Americans, however, there is an immediate connection between the story and the world: "Stories make the world" and "The world is the story."[21] Myths that explain why the badger's tail is long or why the swallows follow the salmon on the Columbia River are more than a series of cause-and-effect statements. At the telling of the myth, the listeners are drawn into the moment of origin so that they become a part of the creation itself. As Frey explains, "It is one thing to tell a story to explain why Coeur d'Alene Lake is *blue*, and quite another to name, bring forth, and participate in the *blue* of Lake Coeur d"Alene through the telling of that story. "And here's the Rock . . . , all blue, just a rollen, just *mad*. And he goes, he goes over the cliff, *down* he goes. And he *rolls* and *rolls*. He goes into the lake. . . ."[22]

In addition to the myths, most of these traditions have countless tales and legends. Like the myths, many of them help explain how things were created and what the interrelationships are between different beings. When these tales are transmitted to the younger people, though, indeed, the older people enjoy hearing them too, they explain the environment and make it more familiar. Many of these tales use a trickster figure to delineate boundaries of proper behavior. Most of the stories, such as the Coyote tales, present things that one should not do in everyday life. For example, Coyote is always complaining about his hunger. When the moment comes that he complains about hunger, people laugh, because they know that you should never complain about that. Coyote is always being carried away by his sexual impulses, and again the listeners laugh because they know that such excesses are unacceptable. Of course eventually, Coyote gets punished for allowing his appetites to run away with him.

A number of things happen in these tales on many different levels. First, there is what you might call the moralistic level. (There is never the punch line that we have in Aesop's fables: "This is what happens if you do this"—the listeners see the point without the narrator's having to emphasize it in that manner.) On this moralistic level, the tales set the parameters for acceptable behavior; they define the limits outside which you are not allowed to go if you are a member of that particular group. Second, on a higher level of understanding, the miraculous events that are a part of the tale remind us that this shifting world of appearances is not really real; there are other levels of reality. For instance, Coyote is tricked into a hollow log and can't get out. Nevertheless, he is able to take a clamshell from behind his ear. He cuts the parts of his body into tiny pieces and throws them out of a knothole; once outside, he puts himself together again. Thus, these episodes help to break the shell of this world of appearances in which we tend to be too set. The rascal/hero character of Coyote helps explain the ambivalence of nature—its tricky character, its seeming reality. Phenomena seem to be real, and yet they are not. As Black Elk used to say to me, "This world is a shadow of another, more real world." This realization, together with the humor, opens up the possibility of participation on other, deeper levels of reality.

Like Coyote, *Iktomi,* the Spider in Lakota, is also a tricky and very clever person. You appreciate why the spider was chosen if you look at all the different types of spiders and their superior hunting skills. Almost all spiders are able to draw out of their own being two different kinds of threads, one smooth and one sticky. When they make their webs, the threads that go in to the center are smooth, but the threads that are in concentric circles are sticky; and, of course, it is the sticky ones that catch the prey.

Within this phenomenon is a positive message for the people, indeed, a spiritual message: so long as you travel to the center, you don't get stuck, trapped, or eaten, but if you go to the right or left, if you diverge from the straight way to the center, you get caught. Thus, the Spider has a positive lesson to teach the people. People also learn from observing that certain types of spiders, when they are hatched out of their eggs, send up little filaments into the air, and when the wind catches these, they are carried for great distances like balloons. People see this as a certain control that the spiders have over the forces of the winds, and this is a power that the people would like to have themselves.

There is a whole range of positive things that one can learn from the Spider. She is thought of as a very industrious person, and this is held up as an example to young girls, because she is always working, weaving, or building. In order to make things more concrete to children, mothers used to stretch ropes and make a kind of spider web between four trees so that it became a hammock, and they placed their children in the middle. The trees were situated according to the four directions of space, and the feeling was that the child would receive powers from the four directions, situated there in the center of the spider web.

The people also look on *Iktomi* as a kind of culture hero who brings important and, indeed, sacred things to the people. The Lakota Sioux, for instance, have a belief that they have never made their own arrowheads out of flint. They find them on the prairie already beautifully made. The belief is that they were made by *Iktomi,* by the Spider, and this is her offering to the people. As far as I know, I have never met a Lakota who knew how to chip an arrowhead out of flint.

They say, "Well, we never had to; the Spider did it for us and we find them in little piles on the prairie and we just pick them up." On the other hand, the Spider can be very, very tricky. Sometimes FBI agents are called *Iktomi*. White people are sometimes called *Iktomi*, because they can be smart and tricky, and you don't know what they are going to do next.

FIVE

"There Is No Word for Art"

The Creative Process

WHEN THE DISTINGUISHED Cape Dorset artist Kenojuak was asked what the word for "art" is, she answered: "There is no word for art . . . we say it is from the real to the unreal, *sanaguatavut.*" James Houston, who has spent the greater part of his life in the Arctic and who was responsible for initiating the new craft of lithography among the peoples of Cape Dorset, in 1957, confirms this statement of Kenojuak with the following: "I believe that Eskimos do not have a satisfactory word for art because they have never felt the need for such a term. Like most other hunting societies, they have thought of the whole act of living in harmony with nature as their art. The small objects that they carve or decorate are to them insignificant reflections of their total art of living." For those of us attempting to understand a culture's world view, such art forms are windows into another people's inner world, and as such they constitute precious documents no less important than the sacred written texts of antiquity. The rich languages of the traditional arts of Native American peoples constitute a range of spiritual perspectives and fundamental assumptions that today are often misunderstood.

One common misunderstanding derives from the separation of art and craft. In Western society, art is generally that which is concerned with aesthetics, while craft is typically thought of as that which is merely functional. To dismiss utilitarian items as being only "crafts" in this way has contributed to the tragic separation of art from life. Within created traditional Native American forms, however, there can be no such dichotomy, because art is not only the particular created form but also the inner principle from which the outer form comes into being. An art form is often seen as beautiful not just in terms of aesthetics but also because of its usefulness and the degree to which it serves its purpose. Since the pre-reservation artist's survival depended on the making of useful things, almost every individual had means by which to manifest artistic ability, and life was permeated and enriched by beautiful forms.

Another common source of misunderstanding pertains to the Western notion of symbol. In Western culture, symbols are generally thought of as formal elements that stand for something else. In contrast, Native American cultures believe the form *is* an actual materialization of the powers, beings, or ideologies represented. When a Navajo singer, for example, ritually creates an image of the *Yei*, or "deity," in a sandpainting, that being or power is understood to be actually present in its visual or material form. When the ceremony is over, the sandpaintings are destroyed, because the Navajo realize that these earthly forms cannot hold the *Yei* for long, and they might not receive their due respect in the daily life outside ritual.

Among the Plains tribes, an animal or a vision painted on a shield or lodge cover is understood to be really present with the fullness of its particular spiritual powers. The powers inherent in these designs are transmitted to the owner of the lodge and the shield bearer. Powers can be transmitted even through highly stylized and abstract representations. In just a single aspect of a depicted being—the paw of a grizzly bear or an elk track—the full force of the entire being may be presented and experienced. In the mythology of all Plains peoples, the porcupine, who climbs high into trees and whose quills radiate from its body, is associated with the sun, the creative principle. The quills that women use to decorate garments, therefore, are identified with and bear the power of the sun's rays. Similarly, elongated fringes and hair on garments can radiate and extend sacred power. Thus, Plains tribes draw from a variety of media that can make spiritual power present.

When the Inuit leave their summer camps on the Arctic shores, many of the stone carvings they have made throughout the season are left behind. While tribal members certainly appreciate the carvings, they consider the process of making them more important than the pieces themselves. Many tribes believe that the artistic process provides a means by which the artist may imitate the Creator who originally created the world. When a Pueblo potter molds a pot from moist clay, she establishes a relationship with the creative force of the earth. She plays the part of the Creator in giving that force a form, and the completed vessel is a living being, both alive and containing life. Similarly, the Tewa weaver participates in acts that imitate the creation of the universe itself. As the following Tewa song reveals, the original creation and artistic human creation mirror each other:

> O, our Mother the Earth, O our Father the Sky,
> Your children are we, and with tired backs
> We bring you the Gifts you love,
> Then weave for us a garment of brightness;
> May the warp be the bright light of morning,
> May the weft be the red light of evening,
> May the fringes be the falling rain,
> May the border be the standing rainbow.
> Thus weave for us a garment of brightness,
> That we may walk fittingly where birds sing,
> That we many walk fittingly where grass is green,
> O our Mother the Earth, O our Father the Sky.[1]

This emphasis on the creative process differs from the Western focus on the finished product. The Navajo erase sandpaintings after ceremonies, while the Western observer may try to capture them in photographs. For the Navajo, the value of the sandpainting is found in its creation and in its use in healing, not in its preservation. The Navajo language reflects this orientation; there are more than 300,000 distinct conjugations of the verb 'to go' and only two or three conjugations of the verb 'to be'. As Gary Witherspoon explains, this seems to point to an emphasis on processes and events, rather than on the static state of being and things. This is expressed in the Navajo sense of beauty, or *hózhó*, which "is not in things so much as it is in the dynamic relationship among things and between man and things."[2] When a Navajo woman made a film about Navajo weaving as part of a cultural study, it was not surprising that the majority of the film showed people moving with sheep over the countryside, searching the hills for herb dyes, and spinning wool. Only a few seconds in the half hour film showed women weaving or the completed rugs. The interaction of people with their environment was shown to be the most artful dimension of weaving.[3]

For the Navajo, the process of creating art offers a way to sustain harmonious relationships. The condition of *hózhó* stretches beyond aesthetics to encompass goodness, happiness, long life, and harmony. For example, some Navajo believe that wearing a juniper seed necklace will prevent them from getting lost in the fog or dark or from having bad dreams. Juniper necklaces are traditionally made from the berries that drop off trees. Chipmunks collect the berries and hide them in their burrows. Navajo children search the countryside for the chipmunk's hideouts, reach in, and take the partially eaten seeds, careful to leave plenty of food behind for the chipmunks. When the seeds are strung together into a necklace, their curative power comes not only from the beads themselves but from the condition of *hózhó* in which they are made. The necklace represents a harmonious partnership among the trees, the animals, and the humans. When this partnership is respected, health and goodness, clarity of vision and freedom from bad dreams are maintained.

Relationships that generate works of art are often highly ritualized. Until as recently as a generation ago, the process of carving Iroquois masks began with a group of men walking together through the forest until the proper tree had been found. At the base of the chosen tree, the carver built a fire, sprinkled tobacco on it, and prayed to the Mask Spirits. The mask was then cut right from the living tree. If the tree continued to live, it meant the power of the tree was now present in the mask itself. Many tribes follow similar ritual prescriptions, believing that the materials of their crafts come from the sacred substances and generative forces of the earth. Prayer, song, sacrifice, and holy pilgrimage must be used to show proper respect to these materials, for when they are properly honored, they may share their life and power with humans.

Woman weaving basket. Photo by Craig Aurness.

These rituals extend into the realm of hunting, especially when an animal's hide is to be used for a ceremonial robe, drum, or shield. For these special objects, many tribes thought—and some still do—that it was inappropriate to puncture the hide of the animal with arrow or bullet. Thus, certain animals such as the deer or antelope were often slain by being run down on foot and ritually suffocated. In this way, the sacred life breath of the animal would be contained within its being. If clothing were to be made from the hide, care would often be taken to honor the animal by not cutting or trimming the hide but leaving it as if it were still the outer clothing of the being that originally wore it. In wearing such a garment or robe, humans would thus partake of the spiritual quality or powers latent in the particular animal. In this vision, all beings and resources of creation were understood to manifest qualitatively differentiated powers, which could be assimilated by humans.

Rituals of preparation help ensure that the art form is a vessel worthy of sacred power. Great care and attention to detail must be given when the work of art has a ceremonial function. The *Yei* and Holy People of the Navajo, for example, will not be coerced into infusing themselves into a sandpainting if the wrong colors are used. The white embroidered kilt worn by impersonators of the Hopi kachinas has changed little since the time the kachinas first visited the Pueblo and gave the people the right to become the powerful kachinas during annual ceremonies. It is important that the kilts be copied faithfully, for it is through the kilts' likeness to their prototype that the spirit of the kachina will become present in the wearer. The kilts also require the accompaniment of the full costume, song, and movement for the transformation process to take place. Thus, each part of the ceremonial whole must be crafted with utmost care. As the preeminent scholar of Sacred Art, Ananda Coomaraswamy, wrote,

> The most immediately significant point . . . is that of the artist's priestly or ministerial function. The original intention of intelligible forms was not to entertain us, but literally to re-mind us; the chant is not for the approval of the ear, or the picture for that of the eye (although these sense can be taught to approve the splendor of truth, and can be trusted when they have been trained), but to effect such a transformation of our being

as is the purpose of all ritual acts. It is, in fact, the ritual arts that are the most "artistic," because the most "correct," as they must be if they are to be effectual.[4]

When something is made in this manner, it is most likely used in a sacred manner in daily life. When a Pomo basketmaker weaves a basket, she passes the grass between her lips to moisten it but also to breathe upon it, to give her life breath into the grass and thus to give to the basket a special sacred quality that remains present in its daily use as a vessel. This fusion of art and life exists today in many tribes. Among the Plains tribes, for instance, most members have a talent for beadwork, tanning, painting, or jewelry making. Every person has the potential to be a special kind of artist, not every artist a special kind of person.

While each individual may have his or her own medium, that which is communicated in traditional art is rarely of a personal, subjective nature. Personal creativity is generally expressed through the traditions and values latent to the tribe. Even when new materials or motifs are adopted by Native American artists, they are quickly absorbed into traditional culture. When the Quakers gave GI blankets to the Navajo, the Navajo unraveled all the blankets and redyed and rewove the wool into the patterns and colors of their own blankets. Today, many Northwest Coast artists produce silk-screen prints, but the images are based on traditional iconography. Within the perimeters defined by tradition, there is room for innovation, though in a manner that is different from the Western avant-garde artist, who may pursue uniqueness for its own sake. The contemporary Haida artist Robert Davidson explains: "Our art has always been in a state of progression. It is a matter of being creative within known and long-established boundaries, but not a matter of being different. Too many people experiment before they have enough knowledge, but that is not innovation. It is bastardization."[5]

Native American art forms emerge from each artist's unique understanding of the world. Since these understandings are often very different from those of Western society, in the words of A. K. Coomaraswamy, "it is not by our aesthetic, but only by their rhetoric" that we can hope to understand and evaluate the art forms of other peoples and other times. There are countless examples from hundreds of tribes that could demonstrate the importance of this process, but, unfortunately, we are limited by space to just a few.

Understanding the images that constitute Native American art can be challenging for the non-Native who is unfamiliar with a tribe's worldview. Eskimo art, for example, is sometimes perceived as abstract and therefore unrealistic. Yet what is perceived as a lack of realism in Eskimo art actually embodies a far deeper reality than physical realism.

68

The Eskimo are acutely aware of the specific traits of the many animals and natural forces they interact with in their homeland. They experience a world peopled with a vast host of spirit beings whose differentiated qualities and associated powers are specific to each form and force of the natural environment. Within this multiplicity, however, the Eskimo perceive a shared spiritual essence at the center of all beings. A well-known story told by the Iglulik and Greenland Eskimo reveals how this shared soul allows humans and animals to be interchangeable.

Once there was a woman who had a miscarriage, and, instead of following the strict taboos for disposing of the fetus, she threw it to the dogs so that no one would know what had happened. The fetus was eaten by a dog, and it remained within the body of the dog for so long that the dog finally gave birth to it. It lived the life of a dog, though it was not very good at pushing in front of the other dogs to get enough to eat. At last it grew tired of being beaten back, so it changed itself into a fjord seal. The soul enjoyed being a seal, but it also wanted to be a wolf for a time. Then it became a caribou, but, since caribou are always afraid, it turned itself into a walrus. Finally, it returned to the body of a seal. One day, it allowed itself to be captured by a man whose wife was barren. The man took the seal home to his wife, and while she was cutting it up, the soul slipped into the woman's body. She became pregnant and gave birth to a healthy son who grew up to be an excellent hunter. And so the woman's miscarried fetus became a human again after dwelling in the bodies of the animals.

Eskimo art reflects this common soul that can be both human and animal. As Edmund Carpenter explains, the Eskimo believe not only in the succession of souls but also in the simultaneity of souls. When a shaman's, or *angákut*'s, soul travels to the Goddess Sedna at the bottom of the sea, his or her soul is joined by the souls of numerous tutelary spirits, such as the walrus, seal, or otter. This is a state of simultaneity rather than transformation, being rather than becoming, and it is eloquently expressed in Eskimo masks and carvings in which lines between humans and animals are lines not of distinction but of fusion. Peter and Jill Furst write, "The same lines serve to depict the continuity of, say, walrus-caribou-man, but when the mask is turned this way or that, or touched in different ways by the dim, flickering light of the dance house, now walrus predominates, now caribou, now the person. At the same time, the other forms contained within the total structure never wholly disappear, for all remain relevant."[6]

Another Eskimo art form, unfortunately referred to as the X-ray image, also reflects the awareness of a shared inner essence. The focus on the internal frees the Eskimo from an overemphasis on outer form. X-ray images do not stop with the outer appearances of beings or things but rather expose forms, often in a highly abstract manner, as if they were transparent, revealing inner structures, vital organs, bones, or any aspect that reflects the shared inner essence of all beings. Similarly, animals in pictographs are often painted with a red line running from their heart and lungs up to their muzzle. These organs are not highlighted in order to depict the physiognomy of the animal. Rather, they reveal the locus of the life-giving breath shared by all beings. In comparison to this inner reality, the outer appearance of the body is almost incidental.

A being, often the Inuit shaman, may be depicted in art forms in a manner that displays, in either realistic or stylized manner, some aspects of his or her essential skeletal structure. Sometimes the shaman, occasionally with skeletal elements exposed, may be depicted inside an animal or animal spirit. For a commentary that exposes the metaphysical sense of these representations, it is difficult to find a more precise statement than that which has been provided by the Iglulik Eskimos as recorded by the great Arctic explorer/scholar Knud Rasmussen:

But before a shaman attains the stage at which any helping spirit would think it worth while to come to him, he must, by struggle and toil and concentration of thought, acquire for himself yet another great and inexplicable power: he must be able to see himself as a skeleton. Though no shaman can explain to himself how and why, he can, by the power his brain derives from the supernatural, as it were by though alone, divest his body of its flesh and blood, so that nothing remains but his bones. And he must then name all the parts of his body, mention every single bone by name; and in so doing, he must not use ordinary human speech, but only the special and sacred shaman's language which he has learned from his instructor. By thus seeing himself naked, altogether freed from the perishable and transient flesh and blood, he consecrated himself, in the sacred tongue of the shamans, to his great task, through that part of his body which will longest withstand the action of sun, wind and weather, after he is dead.[7]

To understand fully the import of this statement, it should be recalled that for all circumpolar peoples, bone is identified with the very source and essence of life. This pervasive circumpolar theme is found to be recapitulated to varying degrees among virtually all native cultures of North, Central, and South America, even among many who are agricultural. Among these peoples, special reverential care is often given to the bones of slain animals. For, if bone is associated with death, it is also life. Life and death, death and life are thus aspects of a single cyclical whole, as hunting people particularly are aware. Translated into the structure of ritual, since there can be no life without death, there is no spiritual life without a spiritual death. Ritual enactments of death and dying, then, are a necessary prerequisite to rebirth, to purification, to a new spiritual life for the initiate. Without participating in this spiritual process, the shaman especially cannot receive those special powers that he or she, as a shaman, must have, live with, and demonstrate through special rites and ceremonies. If we understand this point of view, it becomes clear that the Eskimo's images of skeletons and organs need not be interpreted negatively, as a morbid fixation on death, but are rather a celebration of life, now understood in the sacred sense of rebirth.

The Power Within: Lakota Animal Images

Symbols in traditional Native American art have tremendous significance, for, instead of simply pointing to what they represent, they actually become what they represent. The Lakota Sioux images of animals that appear on shields, tipi covers, robes, and garments provide examples of how this perception of symbols infuses daily life with a sense of connectedness to the Great Mysterious.

The Lakota have a wide base of pragmatic knowledge about how to utilize animals. Yet deeply interrelated with the pragmatic dimension is an inner world of belief and values derived from the animals that gives overall meaning and cohesion to society. The presence of the Great Mysterious is within every being, and even the smallest being, a little ant, for example, can communicate something of the power of the Great Mystery. The bison cow, who gives generously of herself and protects her young by keeping them warm with a red film that spews from her nose, is seen as the Earth, the totality of all that is. The bear, though fierce and deadly, digs deep within in the earth to uncover healing roots and herbs. The quiet, gentle rabbit offers its skin to be worn during the Sun Dance as a model of humility. As Siya'ka, a Teton Lakota man, told Francis Densmore in an interview in the early part of the past century,

All classes of people know that when human power fails they must look to a higher power for the fulfillment of their desires. No man can succeed in life alone, and he can not get the help he wants from men; therefore he seeks help through some bird or animal which Wakan Tanka sends for his assistance. Many animals have ways from which a man can learn a great deal, even from the fact that horses are restless before a storm.[8]

The vision quest was, and still is, one way for Plains men and women to seek out the wisdom of higher powers. Through the physical sacrifice and utmost humility of the three- or four-day vision quest, the individual is opened in a direct manner to contact with the spiritual essences that underlie the forms of the manifested world. Often, the spiritual experience comes in the mysterious appearance of an animal or a winged being, or perhaps in one of the powers of nature. Black Elk explained that "we regard all created beings as sacred and important, for everything has a *wochangi*, or influence, which can be given to us, through which we may gain a little more understanding if we are attentive."[9] Frequently, the animal or bird will share its *wochangi* with the individual during the vision quest, and the *wochangi* will help and protect the person throughout the events of life. When the vision quest is over, the seeker is expected to publicly externalize the experience through a special dance or sacred songs taught him or her by the guardian spirit or through paintings.

Often, young warriors communicated their vision by painting images of their guardian spirits on their shields. Warriors carried these shields into battle, knowing they would protect them, not because the material was indestructible but because the power of the painted animal was present within the shield itself. For instance, a bearer of a wolf shield would be protected by a wolf's fleet movement and knowledge of vast terrain. Also present is the nature of the animal whose hide is used for the shield. A moose is ill tempered and tricky; therefore, a moose shield may help the bearer outsmart the enemy in battle. An antelope is swift and curious, and a shield made from its hide will imbue a warrior with these fine attributes. All the lore related to these animals becomes a part of the art form. Like the rawhide, the paints used for the shield are also considered to have their own inherent powers. Such medicine-paints are carefully prepared from particular types of earth and mixed with special herbs.

Masks can also generate a similar process of identification. After receiving a dream in which the elk spoke to him, Brave Buffalo, a prominent medicine man who lived on the Standing Rock Reservation at the turn of the twentieth century, made an elk mask out of elk hide. He painted himself yellow and carried two hoops wound with elk hide and the herbs that elk enjoy. As he walked around the camp wearing the mask, he thought, "'Now I have done everything as I was directed to do it, and I wish I might show these people that I have the power of the elk. There is a spot of damp ground before me. I wish that when I step on this damp ground I may leave the footprints of an elk.' A crowd of people followed him, and after he had passed over the spot they saw the footprints of an elk instead of a man."[10]

Vision experiences inspired many of the images on tipi covers among most of the Plains tribes. The following vision, experienced by the Blackfeet medicine man Wolf Collar, was also typical of Lakota experiences. During a thunderstorm in the middle of the night, Wolf Collar dreamed that "Thunder, first as a bird, then a woman, took him into her tipi and gave him a drum with four songs. She gave him power to heal people struck by lightning—rub a mixture of yellow paint and wet clay on the person's chest and sing the songs. And said he could paint his tipi like her Blue Thunder Lodge, and with this gave him three songs."[11] After the vision, Wolf Collar painted a yellow Thunderbird on his blue Thunder tipi. He then painted his drum and shield in a similar manner. Only the individual who had received the vision, or someone he had carefully chosen, was allowed to paint the tipi designs, for they were emblems of a special relationship between the vision seeker and the spirit beings.

One particular painted tipi has the image of a bison encircling the dwelling in such a manner that its midsection is positioned over the doorway. This is not simply a bison on the surface, but the bison in full dimension and totality. Upon entering the tipi, one actually enters into the bison. The three-dimensional nature of the tipi adds to the sense that one actually moves into the animal. Though the vision quest begins as an individual experience, something of that experience must be shared with community. Painted tipi covers communicate and share the power derived from an individual vision. Living in such a dwelling allows the seeker and the community to participate continually in a liturgy.

Traditional Lakota ceremonial garments also display the relationships shared between humans and animals, for it is believed that to put on a garment made from an animal is to wrap oneself in the animal's *wochangi*, or power. Often, the *wochangi* is present even in abstract forms. For example, the traditional women's robe, made from the hide of a bison cow, is decorated with a box and border design that depicts, in a highly stylized, abstract manner, all those inner vital and generative life forces of the cow, thus manifesting all that is most sacred to womanhood. To wear such a robe is to participate actively in those forces and to fully experience the sacred dimensions of being a woman. Men's robes, on the other hand, are made from the hides of bison bulls and painted with the sunburst symbols that express the male generative power. The sunburst motif contains the central cross-hatched figure of a stylized sunflower, which during the day always turns to face the sun, the Source of Life. The double-triangle patterns radiating out from the center are the feathers and plumes of the eagle, a solar being, and symbolize the life-giving rays of the sun. The same symbol also represents the cocoon, which contains the potential living form to be released: a moth or butterfly. The entire image speaks both of the creative force of the Great Mysterious and also of all potentiality. Wearing such an art form enriches all dimensions of one's life; a Lakota man wearing this robe may understand and be profoundly influenced by all of these meanings.

"From Me Beauty Radiates": Navajo Weaving

As Native American artists fashion their art out of raw materials, they often follow a pattern of creating that is laid out in their tribe's creation myths. For instance, many scholars contend that Navajo women learned weaving from the Spanish or Pueblos Indians. However, the weavers themselves believe that nearly every step in the process has its source in mythic time. According to Navajo mythology, weaving was taught by Spider Woman, a half-female, half-spider being. One day, long ago, it is said that a young, outcast Kisani woman was walking alone on the prairie when Spider Woman invited her into her home in the ground.

> The girl came down and sat by the Spider Woman who was weaving something. She had a stick about a foot long with a hole in one end like a needle and with this she passed the thread in and out, making the first kind of basket, the Black Design Blanket (*dith-thith-nah-kanê*).
>
> After she had finished what she was weaving, she went up to the top of the ground and, throwing her web up, she pulled the Sun farther to the west and came back. Soon she went up again and pulled the Sun lower until it was almost sunset. Then she told the girl the Sun was low and asked her to stay all night. . . .
>
> The Spider Woman made some dumplings out of grass seeds and fed the girl and the next morning started another loom. She worked so fast that she finished it that day. It was square and as long as your arm and was called Pretty Printed Blanket. The girl watched her all day and stayed there all night, and the next morning the Spider Woman started another loom. She finished this blanket, which she called White Striped Blanket, that day, and on the fourth morning began another. This

Navajo girl feeding lambs. Photo by Jonathan Wilson.

was a 'Beautiful Design Skirt' such as Yeibitchai dancers and Snake dancers wear, and was white with figures in black.

The next morning the Kisani girl went back to the *hohrahn* [*sic*] where she was staying and asked the Navajo for some cotton [this was before sheep and wool] in three colors—yellow, black, and white. After the cotton had been given her, she put up a loom, but not like the Spider Woman's loom. She put it up the way Navajo women do now and began a blanket. Her blanket was about half-done when a Kisani woman came in and looked at the loom and the design. The girl had made a picture of a bird on both sides of the blanket.

"Where did you learn to do that?" the Kisani woman asked.

"I did this on my own thought," answered the girl. "It is called Black Design Blanket."

She finished it in one day, and the next morning she put up her loom again an asked for more cotton to weave. She made a Beautiful Design Skirt the same day. It was finished when two Kisani men came to see what she was doing and asked to see the blankets she had made. One examined the Beautiful Design very carefully, then went home and made another just like it. The girl made only two and then went back to the

Spider Woman's house. The Spider Woman was making a wicker water-jar and after that she made a big carrying-basket such as women carry on their backs. The Kisani girl learned to make the basket and then the water-jar.

"When I went back," she told the Spider Woman, "I showed the people how to make blankets like yours. Now I will go back and make carrying-baskets and water-jars."

"That is good," said the Spider Woman. "I am glad you have taught them. But whenever you make a blanket, leave a hole in the middle the way I do. If you don't, it will bring you bad luck."[12]

The young woman went back to the Navajo and showed them the things she had learned from the Spider Woman. The Kisani men continued to make their blankets, but the Navajo women soon surpassed them as weavers. In Navajo, the word for 'teach' does not translate as "to tell" but literally means "to show," "to describe by action." Navajo women allowed their daughters to watch them herd sheep, spin wool, and weave the blankets. The women passed on the art of weaving in the way that Spider Woman had passed it on to the first Kisani woman, and in this way it has been carried on into the present. Even now, Navajo women use the same teaching techniques. Many also follow this Navajo tradition, in which a spider web is thought to contain the essence of Spider Woman: "When a baby girl is born to your tribe you shall go and find a spider web which is woven at the mouth of some hole; you must take it and rub it on the baby's hand and arm. Thus, when she grow up she will weave, and her fingers and arms will not tire from weaving."[13]

As mentioned earlier, the weaving process begins long before the weaver sits before her loom. Each step is executed with patience and care, few motions without significance or reason. The process starts with the herding and shearing of sheep, which are owned by the women. After the wool is sheared, it must be cleaned, a process in which the wool is painstakingly picked of burrs and twigs and either boiled or soaked in water when available. The wool is then carded by straightening out individual strands of wool through small sharp spikes attached to two "cards," or pieces of wood. It is then ready to be spun and dyed.

The harvesting of plants for dye is given great care. It is said that "after First Man created the mountains and the sky, he invited various People to contribute to the completion and beauty of the earth. Accordingly, the various animals planted the seeds of trees, shrubs, plants, and grasses, which they had brought with them from the lower worlds. There upon First Man breathed on them so that they too might see and live."[14] It is this in-dwelling life force within the plants that lends value to their use in curing ceremonies; the essence remains in the plant after it is picked and remains within the dyes drawn from it. In addition, by using color in a weaving, the corresponding qualities of that color are present in the image. Some colors promote harmony, such as yellow, which is often associated with the West, female qualities, pollen, and growth. Purple, however, is considered dangerous because it is associated with evil beings in myths.

Just as the weaving process was generated in mythic time, so, too, were the first loom and weaving tools. The Moving Upward Chant describes the first loom made by Spider Man in detail:

> The Spider Man drew some cotton (*ndaka*) from his side and instructed the Navajo to make a loom. The cotton warp was made of spider web (*nashjei bitlol*). The upper cross-pole was called *yabitlol* (sky or upper cord), the lowest cross-pole, *nibitlol* (earth or lower cord). The warpsticks were made of *shabitlol* (sun rays), the upper strings, fastening the warp to the pole of *alsinltlish* (lightning), the lower strings of *shabitlajilichi* (sun halo) . . . the cord heald stick was of sheet lightning and was secured to the warp strands by means of rain ray cords.[15]

The loom thus contains all the important elements of creation. It is this model before which the weaver sits, shaping within her loom "world" something of beauty. The original tools used by Spider Woman were also of sacred substance: the warp sticks were made of sun-rays, (*Sha bitlol*), the heald stick of rock crystal (*tsa ghadindini*), the cord heald stick of sheet lightning (*atsolughal*), the batten stick of sun halo (*oljekinaastle*) and the comb of white shell (*yolgai*).[16] Since the tools are identified with these attributes, the weaver is able to touch and have at her command various natural phenomena that are otherwise intangible.

Navajo myth explains that the Holy People thought the world into being. The forms of the world were conceived within the Holy People, and, in mythic time, things actually occurred when people

Navajo weaving lesson. Photo by Jonathan Wilson.

thought about them, because thought, like language, has generative power. This excerpt from a song in the Navajo Creation chant reveals how the Sun was created in First Man's thoughts:

> The sun will be created, they say He is planning it;
> Its face will be blue, they say He is planning it;
> Its eyes will be black, they say He is planning it;
> Its chin will be yellow, they say He is planning it;
> Its horns will be blue, they say He is planning it.[17]

The creation of Navajo art forms follows this movement from inner thought to outer form. Most weavers have their designs carefully planned out in their minds before they start to weave, though they rarely draw the complex designs beforehand. Weavers perfect their conceptions in their thoughts, like First Man of the Holy People, who "thought out" phenomena before creating them. Gary Witherspoon writes:

> The Navajo does not look for beauty; he generates it within himself and projects it onto the universe. The Navajo says *shil hózhó* 'with me there is beauty', *shii' hózhó* 'in me there is beauty', and *shaa hózhó* 'from me beauty radiates'. Beauty is not "out there" in things to be perceived by the perceptive and appreciative viewer; it is a creation of thought. Beauty is not so much a perceptual experience as it is a conceptual one.[18]

When Navajo weavers conceive their designs, they strive for a harmonious balance of form and color. This quest for harmony and order is also of mythological origin. It is said that in the lower worlds, before the time of emergence, First Man and First Woman were inspired to ascend to other worlds by a vision of harmony. As they came up through succeeding worlds, they gained knowledge of the concepts of beauty and balance. For the Navajo, beauty and harmony are realized when the forces of this world are in balance, when evil is overpowered by goodness, illness is restored to health, and disorder is replaced by order. This state of balance, called *hózhó*, is the natural condition of the world. Thus, when a weaver conceives a harmonious design, she is contributing to the overall beauty and goodness of creation. Weaving becomes a vehicle by which *hózhó* is expressed.

Weavers manifest harmony most often through abstract forms. Navajo design reflects little of Western realism, for Navajo tradition is more concerned with inner reality than with the reality of appearances. Geometric and linear forms allow weavers to interpret the world as they perceive it. It is the essence that must be grasped, and abstract forms are most suitable to its manifestation. Instead of limiting the weaver's creativity, these geometric designs, bound by changeless principles, allow for creative expression by virtue of their repetitive, rhythmic, and harmonious nature.

Once the design has been conceived, it must then be manifested. According to Navajo myth, First Man created with his breath, the life force of all living forms. Similarly, the spider creates her web with thread that is drawn from within her being. The web, the product of her creativity, becomes a form away from her but also remains connected to her body. The weaver similarly expresses externally that which is internal, her creative spirit analogous to the thread that brings the fabric "to life." It is this possibility of identification of oneself with the material inherent to the craft that enables the weaver "to put herself into" her weaving. This may explain why the Navajo weaver takes care to not let her spirit be trapped within the fabric. Many women weave a spirit trail leading out of the blanket to provide an avenue by which her spirit, infused into the weaving during its creation, may exit. This practice is not observed by all weavers, and there are varying explanations for its use; all agree, however, that it is not a "path for evil spirits," as some Anglos have called it, but a woven path provided for the good of the weaver.

The Navajo term *yazoni* essentially translates as "that which is beautiful and good" but also pertains to the word *yati*, 'that which is useful'. The traditional weavers' creations are used in both ritual and everyday activity. Not only does woven fabric shelter the Navajo from the elements, but it also has proven to be a profitable industry and contributes to their welfare during times of hardship. The blanket also serves in the ceremonial purposes of curing rites and the blessing of hogans.

The sacred value and mythic genesis inherent to weaving may not be consciously interpreted or abstracted out by the weaver, but she may intuitively sense it. For instance, Pearl Sunrise, a contemporary weaver who also teaches weaving, does not explicitly discuss the sacred nature of her craft, but she does use words such as balance, beauty, and process:

> When you are weave a rug you're not only making an end product. Everything that goes into it is important—the whole process of the work, your thoughts, events that happen while you are weaving. . . . We were taught, "always be busy—use your mind and your hands that are there for you to use creatively. . . . Make it beautiful." [A design] wouldn't be in balance if I just kept on going and creating different things all the way. Everything goes back to the way we were brought up. There has to be balance.[19]

In Navajo weaving, as in the other examples we have discussed, the sacred is comprehended in an experiential and consequently meaningful manner. As a Native American elder eloquently stated: "We do not 'believe' our religion, we live it, dance it."

SIX

Relationship and Reciprocity

A Metaphysics of Nature

Did you know that trees talk? Well they do. They talk to each other and they'll talk to you if you listen. Trouble is, white people don't listen. They never learned to listen to the Indians, so I don't suppose they'll listen to other voices in nature. But I have learned a lot from trees; sometimes about the weather, sometimes about animals, sometimes about the Great Spirit.

—Tatanga Mani, Stoney Indian

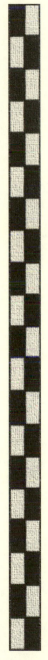

WHEN I FIRST came to live with Black Elk, I was eager to hear him talk about religious matters. All he talked about, though, was animals. Because of my academic background, I kept wondering when he was going to get serious and talk real theology. When was he going to talk metaphysics? When was he going to speak the kind of language I had become accustomed to from Thomas Aquinas? He never did. This was puzzling to me, because I knew he was a man of great sanctity who had experienced the Great Mysterious frequently through visions. Finally, it occurred to me that, in talking about animals and birds, the wind and the four directions, he *was* talking about what non-Natives call "religion." He was, indeed, speaking a sacred, metaphysical language, but it was phrased in terms of living realities in the immediacy of one's experience.

Black Elk could describe his religious experience in this manner, because he, like so many other Native Americans, did not dichotomize human and animal, natural and supernatural. Typical Western distinctions between animism and animatism are not necessarily present in Native American experience, since all forms and aspects of creation are experienced as living and animate. Even "inanimate" rocks are thought to be mysteriously possessed with life. This experience of the sacred does not exclude a unitary, all-inclusive concept that refers to both a Supreme Being and to all gods, spirits, or powers of creation. Black Elk expressed the Lakota understanding of this when he said, "Wakan-Tanka, you are everything, and yet above everything." Abundant recorded materials make it clear beyond any doubt that this type of ultimate affirmation of a Supreme Being was common among most, if not all, Native American peoples well before the coming of white people and Christian missionaries.

When people experience in their daily lives the in-dwelling presence of spirits or "powers" within all forms and forces of the natural world, there is a tendency to treat with reverence all aspects of the environment. This reverence is reflected in a metaphysics of nature that has its roots in a sense of interrelatedness. Unlike the conceptual categories of Western culture, Native American traditions generally do not fragment experience but rather stress modes of interrelatedness across categories of meaning, never losing sight of an ultimate wholeness. Indeed, in Native American religious traditions, humans connect with the Great Mysterious by entering into relationship with its innumerable forms and dimensions. This series of relationships begins with the immediate family and reaches out to encompass the extended family and outward again to the band and the clan and the tribal group. Relationships do not stop with the human but stretch out to the environment: to the land, the animals, the plants, and to the clouds, the elements, the heavens, and the stars. Ultimately, those relationships that people participate in extend to embrace the entire universe.

Associated with relationship is the theme of reciprocity, which permeates so many aspects of North American cultures. Put very simply, reciprocity refers to the process by which, if one receives or takes away, one must also give back. This is a living statement of the importance of the cycle that permeates all of life: the cycle of life and death, of life leading to old age and then coming back to life again. Black Elk so often said that all the forces of the world work in circles: the birds build their nests in circular form, the foxes have their dens in circles, the wind in its greatest power moves in a circle, and life itself is a circle.

Relationships also follow this circular pattern of reciprocity. In treating the world and all its beings in a sacred manner, one is in turn treated well by nature. Black Elk showed me that when a hunter slays an animal, he should thank the animal by blowing tobacco smoke into its nostrils. This act of honor helps ensure the animal's safe passage to the spirit world. It also increases the hunter's fortune the next time he hunts, for the animals know he appreciates the gifts they have given him. Because this cycle is based not on quantitative accumulation but on mutual respect, it generates a profound metaphysics of nature. A sacred pact is forged among all beings of the world, who, instead of emphasizing their material differences, focus on their inherent commonality. The binding force in this pact is the sacred lore held by the people and supported and transmitted by legends, ceremonies, songs, and sense of humility.

The implications of this type of metaphysics of nature are far reaching, given the contemporary underestimation of the sacrality of nature among historical religions. While the awareness of this sacrality was certainly present at the origins of the Judeo-Christian tradition, it has now been forgotten, and, in its absence, our society continues to abuse the natural environment. The earth is viewed as a material commodity that exists to supply the ever increasing, banal needs of an industrial world. Decisions about land management are based on economic value, rather than on the inherent value of the earth. Even elements of the environmental movement approach the earth as an object to be preserved, rather than as a spiritual reality to be respected. This misconception may prove to be fateful, for, as Tonya Gonnella Frichner of the Onondaga Nation has pointed out, "How can you 'save the Earth' if you have no spiritual relationship with the Earth? There is an intellectual abstraction about the environment but no visceral participation with the Earth. Non-Indians can't change the current course of destruction without this connection."[1]

Native American religious traditions, however, have this connection at their core, a core that, if understood at all, has tended to be presented in a kind of romantic, superficial manner by non-Indians. The flip side of the scalping warrior stereotype is the noble savage who worships nature, an image that ignores the sophistication and complexity inherent in most Native American interactions with the natural world. I can remember when Black Elk exploded my romantic notions about these matters. He told me that once, while out hunting, he came across a large group of prairie chickens. It was the time of year when they like to dance in a large circle, strutting and turning and making blowing noises that sound very much like some of the utterances used in the Ghost Dance. I was so enchanted by the image of these singing and dancing birds that I conjured up all kinds of romantic ideas about the lovely relationship between this old man and the beautiful birds of nature. "Well, Grandpa, what did you do then?" I asked. "Oh, I shot them all," he said. I was shocked. He went on to say, "Good eating; they taste good!" I came to understand that within this ideal, close relationship between human and nature that is shaped by sacred values, there is also a pragmatic dimension. That was an important lesson for me to learn. Perceiving the complexity behind romantic stereotypes can help us all understand that a respectful, sacred relationship with the natural world can still be sustaining.

The Roots of Relatedness

Peter Nabokov relays the following story told by Oren Lyons, an Onondaga faith-keeper from New York:

> I was fishing with my uncle, he's an old chief from home, and we were out there in a boat in the middle of the lake and talking about this and that. I had just graduated from college at that point, you know. And I was kind of feeling my oats a little bit. And we were talking and he said, "My you are a pretty smart, you know. You learned a lot of things." I said, "Yeah." I was surprised. And he said, "Good. Then you ought to know who you are then." "Sure," I said. "I am Farland Lyons." He said, "Yeah, that's who you are I guess. Is that all?" . . .
>
> Well, I started thinking. I started to feel a little off track already, and I went to my father's line, my mother's line, my clan. I searched, and he chased me all over that boat for two hours. He wouldn't let me out. I was ready to swim. I was getting mad. Then I said, "Well, who the hell am I then?" And he said, "Well, I think you know, but I will tell you.

"If you sit right here and look right over there, look at that. The rocks. The way they are. The trees and hills all around you. Right where you're on, it's water." And he said, "You're just like that rock." And I listened. He said, "You're the same as the water, this water." I waited and listened again, as he said, "You are the ridge, that ridge. You were here in the beginning. You're as strong as they are. As long as you believe in that," he said, "that's who you are. That's your mother and that's you. Don't forget." I never have.[2]

This story reveals the profound sense of relatedness among all things that characterizes so many Native American cultures. This relatedness not only ties together seemingly disparate beings such as water and rocks but also identifies humans with all of creation. For most Native American culture, the relatedness is rooted in the perception of a shared spiritual reality that transcends physical differences. Some believe this common essence is the life breath; others refer to it as the presence of the Great Spirit. The Seminole are not unique in believing that humans and animals are related because, in the beginning, they were interchangeable. A Seminole/Miccosukee woman, Virginia Poole, a former medical clinic director, says, "We believe that in the beginning, creatures had the ability to change shape—from animal to human, from human to animal.... So we learned that you had to be careful what you said; you never knew if you were talking to a human or animal."[3]

While the exact source of the relatedness may vary, the awareness of it most often developed out of thousands of years of living close to the land. For so long, life depended on the keen observation of natural forms. To survive, people had to discern the behavior and power of natural forces and animals; they had to know such things as which roots cured illness, which bird songs foretold the coming of a storm, and which plants indicated the proximity of underground springs. Through this close interaction between people and the natural world around them, the phenomena of the world were translated into a spiritual language and a metaphysical science that are sustained today. Native American groups have been able to maintain that presiding sense of the sacred that is present in their lands and manifest in all the nonhuman beings. The interrelationships between the nonhumans and the humans constitute a sacred reciprocity and, indeed, a sacred pact.

Bear's Belly, Arikara member of the Bear Clan. Photo by Edward Curtis.

Most Native American cultures have complex understandings of the interrelatedness of all beings. One culture, the Lakota, expresses it succinctly in their most commonly uttered prayer, *Mitakuye Oyasin:* "all my relatives" or "I am related to all that is." All things in the world are related, explains the Lakota artist Arthur Amiotte, because each one has four souls.[4] These four souls are created in the spirit world, where they learn the language of that dimension. When beings become manifest on earth, they maintain the four souls. Thus, rocks, trees, antelope, and humans share a similar metaphysical reality. The first of the shared four souls is called the *Niya*, or the life-breath. The name comes from the word *woniya*, 'that which makes to live' or 'possesses living breath'. The *Niya* infuses all physical forms, whether stone, plant, or animal, with life. During ritual ceremonies such as the Sweat Lodge or the Ghost Dance, a person's *Niya* can leave the body and return to the spirit world, where it interacts with other spirit beings. While the *Niya* is absent, the body may seem lifeless, but, when the *Niya* reenters the physical form, the body is strengthened and purified. The person may even be able to report on the *Niya's* experience of visions or encounters with deceased relatives.

The second soul is referred to as the *Nagi*. This soul is most like the concept of the ghost; it is an individualized, mirror image of the physical form that maintains the idiosyncrasies and personality of its possessor. When young people demonstrate significant knowledge of the world or of a deceased person, they are believed to have the *Nagi* of a person who lived before. Since all *Nagis* are created in the spirit world, they know the same spiritual language. Thus, when a man or woman goes on a vision quest, his or her *Nagi* can communicate with the *Nagi* of animals or forces that become spiritual guardians.

The third soul, the *Sicun*, is the spirit power which all beings possess. Amiotte writes: "For the plant it may be its life-giving fruits, seeds, leaves, or roots or their chemical results as medicines. For animals it may be their unique traits, or the knowledge they have of plants or of celestial and earthy phenomena or behavior, that man desires for himself to help survive. In some animals, it is their possession of the eternal and unfettered wisdom of the gods which man desires to know."[5] *Sicun* is also what gives medicine bundles and ritual objects their power. For instance, if an eagle is ritually killed, its *Niya*, or life-breath, is taken away, but its *Sicun* may still reside in its feathers. The *Sicun* of other beings can be communicated through rituals such as the vision quest and the Sun Dance or through spontaneous vision experiences. If a bear were to visit someone in a vision, a portion of the bear's *Sicun* would be imparted to the person, whose own power would thus be increased.

The fourth and final soul is the *Nagila*, the embodiment of the cosmic energy, or *Taku Skan Skan,* that infuses the entire universe. *Taku Skan Skan* means 'that which moves and causes all things to move'. It is the original source of all things, the divine essence of life. *Taku Skan Skan* is present in each being through the *Nagila*, and it is the sacred thread that binds all things and makes all beings relatives to one another. As Amiotte points out, when we understand the *Nagila*, we can fully grasp the profundity of the prayer *Mitakuye Oyasin.* "We are all related."

These four souls are the basis for the unity of all things. The Lakota also perceive similarities that link seemingly different kinds of beings or phenomena. Western culture often categorizes things by the appearance of their outer form. The Lakota, however, perceive categories on the basis of inner qualities. Beings are placed into categories not on the basis of physical similarity but on the basis of shared, qualitative power. For example, the bison, elk, bear, dragonfly, moth, cocoon, spider, and even cottonwood tree share a unifying element, for all these have certain relationships to the wind or breath. The connection among these unlikely associates starts with the cocoon, for it is from the cocoon that the butterfly or moth mysteriously emerges. The power of the cocoon is thus related to the power of the wind, for neither one can be contained.[6] This relationship is deepened by the wind-producing actions of the wings, a trait also possessed by the dragonfly, which has access to the whirlwind power. Warriors often carried cocoons wrapped in eagle plumes so that they might garner the power of the wind to be elusive, invisible, and destructive in battle.

Another member to be added to this strange assembly of the cocoon, moth, dragonfly, and butterfly is the bison. As with most Lakota conceptions, those concerning the bison are based on careful and pragmatic observation. In winter, when a bison cow drops a calf, she is able to blow out from her nose and mouth a red filmy substance, forming a sack that protects the calf, just as the cocoon protects the developing moth. The bison bull is also included in these associations, for when he is pawing the earth, every now and then deftly scooping up dust and tossing it into the air, the bison is believed to be praying to the Whirlwind to give him power over his enemies. The bull elk is another member in this association, for he has the mysterious power to attract elk cows to him through his whistling call, or "bugle," which again represents control over the air or wind. Men try to identify with this power by using the flageolet to simulate the call of the bull elk. It is believed that this sound is so compelling that young women are irresistibly drawn to the man playing the instrument.

In addition to the large bison and elk, the spider is also related to the wind, for the young of certain spiders send out long filaments that are caught by the wind. The young beings can be carried for long distances on these wind-borne threads. Further concrete expression of this wind relationship is found in the observed fact that at least certain spiders lay their webs on the ground in rectangular shape, with the four corners extended toward the four directions of space, the "homes" of the four winds. Even nonanimals, such as the cottonwood tree, belong to this association. In Lakota, the name for the cottonwood tree is the Rustling Tree, because of its affinity with the wind. The wind blows its leaves and carries the sound of the rustling roar through the air. In season, the cottonwood uses the wind to send out its seeds wrapped in "cotton."

These various beings and phenomena are related not only on an empirical or pragmatic level but also on a sacred level. The abstract, invisible, and synthesizing Wind principle is no other than *Wakan-Tanka*. In *Wakan-Tanka*, the Great Mysterious, all *Wakan* beings coalesce, or fuse without being confused. As Sword, an Oglala Lakota holy man, said, "The word *Wakan-Tanka* means all the *wakan* beings because they are all as if one."[7] Even though Western culture distinguishes the cottonwood—a tree—from the bison—an animal— the Lakota see them as unified in the power of the Wind, and thus in *Wakan-Tanka*. Therefore, each of these beings is treated with respect and appreciation. The unifying characteristics of these seemingly disparate beings define human interactions with them: cocoons are coveted and valued; the bull elk is studied and emulated; the bison cow is a model of nurturing motherhood. For the Lakota, intercepting the horizontal dimension to the world of appearances, there is always this vertical dimension of the sacred that connects all beings in relationship.

Within the unity of things, however, there is a hierarchy of power. For instance, the origin myths tell us that animals were created before humans beings, and in their anteriority and their divine origin they have a certain proximity to *Wakan-Tanka* that demands respect and veneration from humans. While all animals have *Sicun*, or spirit power, to share, some have more than others; this is more of a qualitative difference than a quantitative one. The bison is chief over all the animals of the earth, for in its generosity, strength, and support of Lakota life it represents, as Black Elk said, "the earth, the totality of all that is." It is the eagle, however, who is considered to be most sacred, and spiritually the most powerful, of all living nonhuman beings. Since it is the eagle who flies higher than all other wingeds, the eagle is associated with the sun, and eagle feathers are thought of as the sun's rays. It is because of these sacred solar associations that headdresses and trailers are made from eagle feathers and that, in Sun Dance ceremonies, the dancers continually blow on whistles made from the wind bones of the eagle.

There is also a hierarchy between the hunter and hunted, as the story of the Great Race tells us. The Great Race took place on a race course that surrounds the Black Hills of South Dakota. Indeed, in flying over the Black Hills once, I noticed that there are traces of a strip around the base of the Black Hills where the race had taken place. The race on that course emerged out of a problem: the peoples, which means all humans and animals, were living in a great deal of anxiety, because it was never clear who had the right to eat whom. Was it, as it was said, that the four-legged beings have the right to eat the two-legged animals, or did the two-legged animals have the right to eat the four-legged beings? This caused a certain tension and uncertainty, so it was decided that this matter should be resolved through a race. All the beings were to gather at an appointed time at the beginning of the race course. All the animals came, and the race was started.

Now, as the animals ran against each other, each one tried to put the others out of commission by practicing magic against them. The buffalo, however, runs with his great head down, and he doesn't look right or left. So he did not get distracted by anything and was impervious to the workings of magic against him by the other animals.

And, indeed, he was well ahead. The buffalo had come almost to the finish line when, all of a sudden, a magpie who had been sitting between the horns of the buffalo jumped out from between the horns and, in magpie fashion, swooped ahead and crossed the finish line first of all. And so it was that the magpie, who is a two-legged being, won the race. It was then decided that forever afterward, the two-legged beings, which includes humans, have the right to eat the four-legged beings, such as the bison, the deer, and so on. As a reward for winning the race, the Great Judge, maybe *Wakan-Tanka* himself, gave the magpie a rainbow to wear. And so it is to this day, if you look at a magpie, you will notice that in the feathers of his tail, there are the multicolored radiating feathers that remind you very much of the rainbow.

Humans have a unique position in the hierarchy of beings. While each animal reflects particular aspects of the Great Spirit, human beings include within themselves all the aspects. A human being is thus a totality, bearing the Universe within. Nonetheless, humans must rely on the animals and the forces of nature to become aware of their full potential. As Black Elk said: "Peace . . . comes within the souls of men when they realize their relationship, their oneness, with the universe and all its powers, and when they realize that at the center of the Universe dwells *Wakan-Tanka*, and that this center is really everywhere, it is within each of us."[8]

Animal Beings as Teachers

In animals, many Native Americans see actual reflections of the qualities of the Great Spirit, which serve the same function as revealed scriptures in other religions. They are intermediaries or links between human beings and God. This explains not only why religious devotions may be directed to the deity through the animals but why contact with, or from, the Great Spirit comes to Native Americans almost exclusively through visions and communications involving animals or other natural forms. This phenomenon is found throughout Native America. For instance, Aua, an Iglulik Inuit shaman, told Rasmussen in the 1920s that he attributed his powers of healing to a shark who spoke to him while he was kayaking.[9] In the Plains, Magpie on Earth, a Crow woman who lived at the turn of the century, was led by a chickadee to a place where she saw four jack rabbits building sweat lodges. They told her to build four similar lodges, start fires in each one, and make four smudges. "If you do this," she was told, "and you desire something, it will come to you easily."[10]

Since many cultures perceive animals to be sent by the Great Spirit, traditional people relate to the nonhuman beings of the land, water, and air as their teachers. Each of these beings is understood to be endowed with specific sacred qualities and powers that can be communicated to the human person. Thus humans enter into relationships with the beings in an effort to receive knowledge and power. These relationships must be highly respectful, for, as many of the songs, myths, rites, and art forms illustrate, animal beings are not lower, that is, inferior to humans. Rather, because they were here first in the order of creation, and with the respect always due to age in these cultures, the animal beings are looked to as guides and teachers of human beings—indeed, in a sense, as superiors.

In many Native American traditions, animals actually assisted the Creator in completing the world, and many of the animal creators show a benevolent concern for humans. The Salish believe that the tricksters Coyote and Fox passed through the Bitterroot Valley (in present-day Western Montana) before humans arrived, to prepare the ground for the Bitterroot Salish tribe. Similarly, many Pueblo creation myths explain that when humans emerged from the dark underworld, it was the animals who helped them climb into the land of the sunlight. The poor humans, some Pueblo myths say, had no eyes or mouths, so the animals cut slits in their faces so that they could see, talk, and eat. There are many more such examples that illustrate the awareness that animals are willing to help us in this world.

Animals often act as guardians, watching over humans and intervening when necessary. The Pawnee, for example, tell of a sacred, dome-shaped hill called *Pahok* that rests on a high bluff above the Platte River in eastern Nebraska. Within this hill is a large circular chamber where representatives of all the animal and avian beings are gathered in permanent session. This council of animals is called *Nahurac*, and it continually monitors the actions and thoughts of human persons. When the animals see that a particular person is in great difficulty or is seeking a vision experience, the council discusses the matter and decide which of the animals or birds possess the powers that could help the person. That being appears to the human in need and offers him or her power and guidance.

While most animals are generous with their knowledge, many cultures believe that it is the responsibility of humans to keenly observe the ways of animals. Through careful study of animal behavior, humans can come to understand the nature of their power. As the Lakota Brave Buffalo said, "Let a man decide upon his favorite animal and make a study of it, learning its innocent ways. Let him learn to understand its sounds and motions. The animals want communicate with man, but *Wakan-Tanka* does not intend they shall do so directly—man must do the greater part in securing an understanding."[11] Before the reservation era, learning to study animals was the major component in the development and education of young people. Parents encouraged their children to be attentive, to be ever watchful of the animal and plant inhabitants of their environment. This tradition is passed on today, as is evident from the words of Arvol Looking Horse, The Keeper of the Sacred Pipe of the Lakota Sioux: "We also learn how to take care of ourselves by learning from the animals—even the prairie dogs. We can tell how high the snow banks will be that winter by how high they build their homes. We also believe that how much you put into something is how much you will receive in return. So it's a really good life when you look at it that way. We learn from the animal nation."[12]

For many Native American cultures, living in close understanding with nonhuman beings is essential to becoming fully human. For humans to become what we are, we need the possibility of contrasting ourselves with nonhuman beings. Each animal has qualities that are counterparts to qualities within the human soul, and it is only through attentiveness to animals that we can come to realize all these aspects within our own selves. For examples, the Lakota have observed that the red-throated woodpecker listens very carefully when it searches for food within a tree. People encourage their children to notice this trait, for it is also important for humans to be attentive to the messages around them. Through this type of intense and frequent contact with the powers and qualities of the animals and, eventually, all forms of life, humankind is awakened to, and thus may realize, all that an individual potentially is as a human person. Human completion, wholeness, or religious awakening depends on this receptive opening up to the potentialities and sacred mysteries in the immediate natural environment.

Over time, the animal qualities that help humans meet their potential have become encoded into the value system of many Native American cultures. Animal traits are studied and observed not simply because they may help in food gathering or healing but also because they express admirable values toward which humans may strive. When a bison calf is orphaned, the cows of the herd immediately adopt it. They shower the calf with care and affection by licking its coat with their rough tongues until the calf's hair becomes as fine and silky as a beaver skin. The Lakota respect this display of nurturing and have translated it into their own culture. All children are raised by many clan members. Sometimes, however, one child may show signs of great potential as a quill worker, a warrior, or a healer. He or she is designated as one who will receive extra attention, knowledge, and gifts. Thus, following the example of the bison cows, the Lakota sustain and encourage the unique child.

Many Northwest Coast cultures also try to emulate the traits of animals. Among these tribes, entire clans are identified with the qualitative aspects of one specific animal. The animal is most often painted around the doorway to the clan house so that, as one enters the house, one enters into the spirit animal that dominates the clan. In addition to the visual representation of esteemed animal traits, many cultures rely on animal-inspired stories, clothing, and movements to invoke the power of specific animals. These powers help carry and support the sacred values, moral norms, and ethical procedures that constitute what it means to be human.

The Reciprocal Cycle

The relationships that Native American traditions sustain with nature are cyclical. Humans gain power, knowledge, and life from animals and natural forces, and in turn they give respect, honor, and appreciation. The values that support this balance are embedded within the interactions among humans, animals, plants, and elements. For instance, part of the cycle of life inevitably entails death; in order to live, people must take the life of other beings. Within most Native American cultures, however, the life of an animal or plant is seen as a gift that must not be taken for granted, or it will no longer be offered. As Richard Nelson tells us, the Koyukon of Northwestern Alaska believe that the spirits of the natural world "are especially watchful for irreverent, insulting, or wasteful behavior toward living things. The spirits are not offended when people kill animals and use them, but they insist that these beings (or their remains) be treated with the deference owed to the sources of human life."[13]

A complex system of rules and prescriptions has been passed down so that the Koyukon will know how to relate respectfully to the natural world. Hunters are told not to boast about hunting bears, for all the bear spirits will be offended by this arrogance and will not allow themselves to be caught. Wounded animals must be treated humanely; for instance, a moose stuck in deep snow might be fed until it is able to get free. Bones of water animals, such as beaver, muskrat, and mink, should be placed back into a body of water.[14] There are significant consequences for not following the proper taboos. Bad luck in hunting, illness, clumsiness, or even death may occur when people do not attend to animals respectfully. Fur animals are easily offended by noise and bad smells, and one hunter recalls: "I had bad luck with fox this year. Come to think of it, I was using noisy power tools while I had a [body of a] fox in the house. Guess that's why . . . it's got really sensitive ears."[15]

This ethic of honor extends to plants, as well as to animals. Most interactions with plant beings stress the understanding that when one has been given to, one must give back. If a person acts selfishly and offends the spirit of a healing root or bark, then that spirit will no longer offer itself. Thus, a respectful demeanor toward plant beings ensures future good relations. Pacific Northwest basket makers are careful to pray to the tree whose bark they are going to take. As the contemporary Lummi basket maker Fran James says, "We tell him we're not going to abuse him. If the tree doesn't believe you, you get into trouble."[16] The following is a traditional Kwakiutl basket maker's prayer:

> Look at me, friends!
> I come to ask for your dress,
> For you have come to take pity on us;
> For there is nothing for which you cannot be used . . .
> For you are really willing to give us your dress,

I come to beg you for this,
Long-Life maker,
For I am going to make a basket for lily roots out of you.
I pray you, friend, not to feel angry
On account of what I am going to do to you;
And I beg you, friend, not to feel angry
On account of what I am going to do to you;
And I beg you, friend, not to tell our friends about what I ask of you.
Take care, friend![17]

The Seneca tribe of the Northeast believe that one of the most important ways of paying respect is through gratitude and thanksgiving. In the following prayer, they give thanks to their sisters: corn, beans, and squash:

Those who take care of [the corn, beans, and squash] every day asked, too, that they be sisters. And at that time there arose a relationship between them: We shall say, "the Sisters, our sustenance," when we want to refer to them. And it is true: We are content up to the present time, for we see them growing. And give it your thought, that we may do it properly: We now give thanks for the Sisters, our sustenance. And our minds will continue to be so.[18]

Honoring of plant spirits in this way automatically fosters an ethic of conservation, for one would not exhaust the spirit of a respected being. Many Native American cultures believe that humans must assist the world in its ongoing creative process; therefore, they should help sustain the life of the planet by not wasting anything. Thus, they perform the rituals and prayers that will encourage the plants to continue growing.

Respectful interactions with nature are more than choreographed steps or empty rituals. For Black Elk, a bird like the eagle was not arbitrarily a symbol of some other or higher reality; it was that reality manifest. I learned this lesson in a hard way. In the 1940s, I joined Lakota people in hunting eagles. Elders valued eagle feathers for headdresses and plumes, wing bones for the Sun Dance whistles, and claws for necklaces. Black Elk appreciated receiving these forms for use in various rites himself. Yet, one day he said to me: "Do not shoot eagles, for you will be shooting me." In his frequent vision-encounters with the eagle, he had come to identify with all that the eagle represented. Furthermore, because of the eagle's many virtues, including its ability to fly in circles toward the sun, he understood the eagle to be ultimately none other than the Great Spirit. The eagle formed a link between Black Elk and the Great Spirit. Thus, Black Elk related to each eagle as he would relate to the Great Spirit itself.

Human completion, wholeness, or religious awakening depends on this type of constant, receptive opening up to the relatedness and the sacred mysteries of the immediate natural environment. Once, when Black Elk and I were traveling to Denver, we were overtaken by a terrible storm. We had to stop driving, because the road was about to be washed out. Black Elk quietly took his pipe and got out of the car. He lit the pipe, chanted softly, and soon the sky cleared. It seems that his relationship to nature included the forces of thunder and rain. He was able to work with these forces toward a beneficial result. Black Elk was an extraordinary man, but interrelationship with nature is encouraged among all peoples within Native American traditions. It is something that pervades all aspects of life, every day. As Carole Anne Heart Looking Horse, a Lakota lawyer and educator, says: "I keep tobacco in my car. When Chante and I are out driving down the road, if we see a little animal that got run over, we stop and offer tobacco and say a prayer for the animal's spirit. If you believe in the Way of the Pipe, you try to incorporate spiritual ways into every minute of your life."[19]

A Delicate Balance

The values supported by the Native American metaphysics of nature have implications for the modern world, for they offer an example of what Western culture sadly has lost or forgotten. While some non-Natives are beginning to learn from these values, many have been blinded to them because of non-Natives' profound misunderstanding of Native American cultures. Since the initial contact between Native Americans and Europeans, we have seen take place a tragic drama of two cultures in conflict, each representing to the other diametrically opposed values on every possible level and in all domains. This is perhaps most clearly exemplified in the notion of Manifest

Destiny, which embodied the European-American values of industrial progress and the private ownership of land for the exploitation of natural resources.

Agriculture was the flagship of Manifest Destiny, for European-Americans identified it with civilization. Many of the historically nomadic Native American tribes, however, found commercial, large-scale farming contradictory to their value systems. Some viewed the earth as sacred and inviolate and not to be torn up with a plow. The famous words of Smoholla, a Nez Perce holy man, expressed this belief:

> You ask me to plow the ground. Shall I take a knife and tear my mother's breast? Then when I die she will not take me to her bosom to rest.
>
> You ask me to dig for stone. Shall I dig under her skin for bones? Then when I die I cannot enter her body to be born again.
>
> You ask me to cut grass and make hay and sell it and be rich like white men. But how dare I cut off my mother's hair?[20]

In order to grasp the indignation that inspired this type of statement, one need only visualize early farming practices from the Native American point of view. Plains tribes were scandalized by the way nineteenth-century homesteaders, after diminishing the bison population from 70 million to 256 within a few decades, proceeded to plow up acres and acres of ground to work the top soil. Native Americans were convinced that little good could come from turning the soil the "wrong side up," and indeed, when the drought of the 1930s hit the Plains, the top soil blew away, and people and animals starved. Tens of thousands of settlers fled the Great Dust Bowl, leaving behind their deserted farmhouses and their impact on the land.

While Native Americans did not respect Anglo farming practices, European-Americans had a deep prejudice against the nonagrarian, nomadic, or pastoral peoples. European-American culture concluded that, because tribes did not build towns, till their fields, or domesticate their animals, they must be unwilling or incapable of "real" work. Government agents and missionaries launched a campaign to "civilize" the Native Americans through agriculture. In 1887, Congress passed the Allotment Act, which declared that all tribal land must be broken into privately owned parcels for cultivation. Complaining about the evils of communally held lands, the bill's sponsor, Senator Henry Dawes, proclaimed, "There is no selfishness, which is at the bottom of civilization. Till this people will consent to give up their lands, and divide them among their citizens, so that each can own the land he cultivates, they will not make much more progress."[21]

Many Native Americans, on the other hand, viewed the results of the European-American way of life and decided they wanted no part of it. In the early 1960s, a picture of a deserted farmhouse in a gullied field appeared in a farm publication with a prize offered for the best 100-word description. A Native American took the prize with this:

> Picture show white man crazy. Cut down trees. Make big tipi. Plow hill, water wash. Wind blow soil. Grass gone. Door gone. Window gone. Whole place gone. Buck gone. Squaw gone. Papoose too. No chuck-away. No pigs. No corn. No plow. No hay. No pony. Indian no plow land. Great Spirit make grass. Keep grass. Buffalo eat grass. Indian eat Buffalo. Hide make tipi; make moccasin. Indian no make terrace. All time eat. No hunt job. No hitch-hike. No ask relief. No shoot pig. No build dam. No give dam. Indian waste nothing. Indian no work. White man crazy.[22]

Underlying Native American resistance to the exploitation of land is the understanding that the natural world sustains its own balance. This balance consists of a series of interrelationships. For the Plains tribes, there are chains in which the grass feeds the vole, who feeds the skunk, who feeds the eagle. Seeds feed the prairie deer mouse, who feeds the weasel, who feeds the coyote. The basic chemicals of life are constantly recycled through these relationships. However, this balance can easily be upset. Removing sage brush to make room for more grass ends up leading to the opposite effect, since broom weed can come in and dry out all the grass and contribute to erosion.

Most tribes have a sophisticated understanding of the ecosystems of their regions, yet time and again, they have witnessed non-Natives come into their land and act without regard to those systems. In the 1950s, the Bureau of Land Management (BLM) decided that large areas of New Mexico and Arizona were infested with gophers. The gophers dug holes that tripped livestock, so a plan was designed to eradicate the pests. The Navajo of the area protested the plan, claiming it would affect the entire region. The BLM paid little heed to these warnings and proceeded to poison, trap, and eliminate the gophers. In no time at all, the sections of the prairie where the gophers had lived became desolate and sandy, and indigenous plants died off. The grass simply stopped growing. It became obvious that the gophers' holes had somehow allowed the water to penetrate and nurture the soil. The BLM had neglected to take into account the essential role the gopher played within the delicate balance of the region. In their attempts to improve the grazing conditions, they destroyed them. They later fenced off an area to test this connection, and the same thing happened; they had a near desert in a short period of time.

It is through such examples that the meaning of the Lakota prayer *Mitakuye Oyasin*, 'We are all related', once again becomes clear. An environmental ethic based on an understanding of sacred interrelationship does more than work to protect the material forms of nature. It also encompasses the understanding that when the wild lands are compromised—as they are all across the country—then the values identified with the land, and the sacred meanings of the different animals, are also compromised irrevocably. This is what we must consider when we discuss large-scale degradation such as toxic waste dumps, open pit mining, and clear cuts. Janet McCloud, a direct descendant of Chief Seattle and a spokesperson for Northwest Coast Nisqually fishing rights, reminds us: "There's an energy in the universe that links us to all other life forms. We are all children of the Earth. We have these earthquakes and other natural disasters because people are poisoning their Mother the Earth, they are poisoning her bloodstreams and cutting off her hair. They're not following the living laws about caring for the Earth. . . . We need to value life, we need to find joy in it, and give something back."[23]

"All the Creatures We Kill Have Souls":
The Iglulik and Sedna

When humans let their relationship with the natural world get out of balance, they can turn to rituals to restore it. The journey of Iglulik

Eskimo shamans to visit Sedna, the Mother of the Sea Beasts, is an example of how the many different dimensions of a metaphysics of nature can come together in a ritual ceremony. The Iglulik believe that all beings have the same kind of soul. While this represents a level of closeness, it also represents an element of danger. Ivaluardjuk, a Iglulik who spoke with Knud Rasmussen in the 1920s, voiced his tribe's concerns: "The greatest peril of life lies in the fact that human food consists entirely of souls. All the creatures that we have to kill and eat, all these that we have to strike down and destroy to make clothes for ourselves, have souls, like we have, souls that do not perish with the body, and which must therefore be propitiated lest they should revenge themselves on us for taking away their bodies."[24]

In addition to the souls of each animal, Iglulik must also worry about offending Sedna, the guardian of all animals. There are different versions of the story of Sedna, but most of them recall that when Sedna was a young woman of the land, she refused to marry the man her father had chosen for her and ran off with a stranger. Once the two were at sea, the new husband revealed himself to be a stormy petrel in human form. Sedna burst out crying when she discovered she had married a bird, but she went away with him to a nice, warm home, where they had a child. Soon, Sedna's father began to miss his daughter. One day, he paddled out to retrieve her while her husband was hunting. When the husband returned and found his wife gone, he flew out to sea to find the fugitives.

As the bird swooped down on the boat, the father tried to protect Sedna from being taken away. But he grew so fearful of the angry bird-husband that he tried to throw Sedna into the water. But Sedna clung to the boat. Her father took a knife and hacked off the top joints of her hand. The joints bobbed into the water and turned into seals. Still, Sedna grasped onto the boat. Her father hacked off the next joints, and these fell into the water and became bearded seals. And still Sedna hung on. Finally, her father hacked off the last joints, and these turned into walruses. Now Sedna could no longer hold on. She slipped off the boat and sank to the bottom of the sea, where she watches over the children of her hands, the sea beasts, and, according to some, the land beasts, as well. After Sedna was gone, her father grieved so much that he, too, was drawn to the bottom of the sea. When humans are being disrespectful to her animals, Sedna calls them to her sea home, where they stay until humans mend their ways.

An extensive system of requirements and taboos helps prevent the Iglulik from offending Sedna and the animals' souls, but the rules are often transgressed. People waste food, they forget to offer a last drink of water to the soul of a hunted seal, or women refuse to tell the village when they have miscarriages. When things like this occur, the weather gets bad. The game disappears, and the source for food, clothing, and fuel is gone. Fortunately, shamans are able to have their souls leave their bodies, so they can travel to the bottom of the sea to placate Sedna. To become a shaman, a pupil must fast and isolate himself or herself for long periods of time. Most important, a shaman must introduce the initiate to the helping spirits by withdrawing, in a mysterious manner, the pupil's soul from his or her eyes, brains, and entrails. In this way, the spirits come to recognize the noblest aspect of the initiate, and the new shaman becomes accustomed to traveling outside his or her body. The Eskimo K. J. Butler hinted at the scope of those travels by saying, "When the moon rocket went to the moon and some of the young kids were trying to tell the old people about this, they were getting really frustrated because the old people were saying, 'Oh, that's nothing, my uncle went to the moon lots of times.'"[25]

Perhaps a shaman's most important journey, however, is to the depths of the ocean. If an individual is sick or having poor luck hunting, or if the whole village is threatened by starvation, shamans hold a ceremony in the almost utter darkness of a hut. The shamans ask their helping spirits to clear the way to the sea; when the spirits arrive, they make an opening in the earth beneath the shamans through which they slowly sink. The spectators hear the shamans' voices recede, and they know that they are now facing the obstructions that are placed in the path to Sedna: large stones, a vicious watch dog, and Sedna's angry father. Finally, once the shamans enter her home, they can see Sedna, sitting with her back to the light, her hair tangled with the dirt and slime of human wrongdoing. She is practically suffocated by the impurity. Gently, the shamans take a comb and draw it through the hair Sedna can not comb because she has no fingers. The shamans soothe her anger and tell her that people on land are ailing or that the animals have disappeared.

Sedna responds by telling the shamans the specific offenses that humans have committed. After the shamans cajole her and assure her that the humans will change, she lets the animals go one by one. Now the shamans can return to the hut and to their bodies. The shamans will then imply that they know what has affronted Sedna but wait for the people themselves to tell of their transgressions. There is an outpouring of confession until the main person responsible for the trouble finally admits what he or she has done. Rasmussen noted that this declaration is followed more by joy and relief than by condemnation, for, now that the source of Sedna's anger is out in the open, the people can restore balance, and the game and good weather will return.[26]

Ceremonies such as this support sound ecological practices, for they remind humans that, when they offer respectful treatment to animals, the animals will continue to offer themselves to humans. This cycle of reciprocity is regenerative: the vow to use almost every part of a caribou ensures that there will always be caribou, for people will not have to kill another animal for each new need. Killing in this type of ritualized context guarantees that resources will be renewed, and life will continue. While the Eskimo world includes the perilous reality of killing other souls, it also contains the experience of joyful harmony. Here is but one of the many Eskimo songs that are referred to as "Songs of Joy":

> When I am out of the house in the open,
>   I feel joy.
> When I get out on the sea on haphazard,
>   I feel joy.
> If it is really fine weather,
>   I feel joy.
> If the sky really clears nicely,
>   I feel joy.
> May it continue thus
>   for the good of my sealing!
> May if continue thus
>   for the good of my hunting!
> May it continue thus
>   for the good of my singing-match!
> May it continue thus
>   for the good of my drum-song![27]

SEVEN

A Unity of Experience

Purification, Expansion, and Identity through Ritual

NATIVE AMERICAN RELIGIOUS traditions stress a unity of experience. Where such traditions are still alive and spiritually viable, the dimension and expression of the sacred is present in all of life's necessary activities. When the elements of time, place, language, art, and the metaphysics of nature come together, however, as they do in ritual activities, the experience of the sacred is intensified. Such ritually generated sacred power flows beyond the immediate participants, to nourish and sustain the entire world.

Despite forecasts that they would become fully assimilated into mainstream culture, Native Americans continue to practice rituals that embody their traditional values. Koyukon potlatches, Lakota giveaways, Crow Sun Dances, Zuni Shalakos, and the Seminole Green Corn Ceremonies are just a few of the thousands of rituals that thrive throughout Native America today. The vitality of these traditions demonstrates tremendous persistence, considering the fact that religious freedom was actively denied to Native Americans for much of the past two centuries. The following decree, issued by the Indian Commissioner to the Blackfeet in 1894, is typical of the countless prohibitions against Native American religious practices: "Sun dances, Indian mourning, Indian medicine, beating of the tom-tom, gambling, wearing of Indian costumes . . . selling, trading, exchanging or giving away anything issued to them have been prohibited, while other less pernicious practices, such as horse-racing, face-painting, etc. are discouraged."[1] Even in the face of such restrictions, Native Americans managed to sustain their rituals by keeping them secret from outsiders, moving them to remote places, or simply disguising them as Fourth of July celebrations.

Today, federal laws pose further threats to Native American religious freedom. Numerous Supreme Court decisions make it exceedingly difficult for Native Americans to protect sacred lands from logging , dam projects, and interpretive tourist centers. Industrial activity on sacred lands often prevents tribal members from undergoing vision quests, hunting for ceremonial purposes, and gathering healing herbs. At worst, it extinguishes the spirits who live in the land, rendering the land lifeless and gutting tribal traditions. In addition to sacred land disputes, Native American face restrictions on their traditional practices. Until 1995, the use of peyote for Native American Church ceremonies was considered a felony in twenty-two states. Native American inmates are routinely denied the right to pray by burning sweet grass or to speak with tribal holy people, though their Christian counterparts receive communion and visit with ministers.

Nonetheless, tribes have entered the courts themselves and have succeeded in regaining some of the rights of religious freedom enjoyed by most Americans. In 1990, Congress passed the Native American Graves Protection and Repatriation Act, which requires federally funded museums and universities to give tribes an inventory of all human remains, medicine bundles, and sacred materials in their holdings and to promptly return the pieces to the appropriate tribes. Thanks to the efforts of Native American religious freedom organizations, President Bill Clinton issued an executive order in 1994 that protects Native Americans' right to possess eagle feathers. In 1995 Congress passed a law legalizing the use of peyote for Native American Church members in all states. However, when Senator Daniel Inouye (D-Hawaii) brought the Native American Freedom of Religion Act before the Congress in 1995 in an effort to strengthen past religious freedom bills and to protect sacred lands, the bill was rejected. Competing mining and timber interests and the American reverence for private property make it very difficult to gain protection for sacred lands. Many tribes are turning to the United Nations and international human rights court for support.

Center pole, Crow Sun Dance Lodge, Montana. Photo by Marina Weatherly.

On a deeper level than the legal platform, Native Americans traditions are sustained by the understanding that culture is dynamic. New ideas and innovations may be incorporated into a culture without diminishing its core values. A Navajo may go to a medical clinic for certain illnesses and have a chantway performed for others. Now that there are no longer war or hunting ceremonials on the White Mountain Apache Reservation, the girls' puberty rite, *na ih es*, has taken on a new significance for the entire tribe. In addition to traditional blankets, the gifts at an Koyukon potlatch may now include housewares and appliances.

Christianity is yet another thread that has been woven into Native cultural fabric. For many Native Americans, contact with Christianity is more of an adhesion than an exclusivist conversion. There are certainly extremes among tribal members, those who reject Christianity and those who adopt it exclusively, but there is also an even larger group that is situated in a unique manner between the two. Running through virtually all indigenous Native American traditions is the pervasive theme that the sacred mysteries of creation may be communicated to humans through all forms and forces of the immediately experienced natural environment. Such openness of mind and being toward manifestations of the sacred has made it possible for Native Americans to adopt and adapt the Christian expression of values into the fabric of their own religious cultures. Black Elk, for instance, was willing and able to be a catechist and still participate in the rites of the Sacred Pipe and the shamanistic Yuwipi ceremonies. If this process of synthesis can be accomplished with neither confusion nor dissonance, it is ultimately because of the ability of Native American people to penetrate and comprehend the central and most profound nature of all experience and reality.

Even with modern additions and adaptations, however, authentic rituals remain firmly rooted in mythic tradition. Most sacred rites practiced today originated in mythic time. They are present at the center of the cosmos; they are part of the changelessness at the center of change. Implied in this is the assumption that neither the myth nor the supporting ritual is ultimately of human origin. Indeed, within the traditions in question, they are always of suprahuman origin. The Midwinter ceremony of the Iroquoian people is an example of such a ritual. The ceremony was originally ordained by the Creator, Sky-Holder, so that when the new year is ushered in, the healing power of old dreams and the warmth of old fires can be rejuvenated. In the following Onondaga creation myth, the Creator tells how He modeled the four rites that constitute the Midwinter ritual after mythic ceremonies:

> I myself too will regard as an important matter what I will leave here on the earth, the Four Ceremonies, or Rituals. . . . I have patterned it after the ceremony as it is being carried on in the place where the Earth, which you call the Sky, is. And it is actually so, the pleasure with which those in the upper side of the sky rejoice is most important. I patterned it so because I desire that the ceremonies that will be going on here on earth, on the under side of the sky, shall be the same as those.[2]

If ritual acts do not derive from and express the sacred in this way, if they are not consciously participated in, then the actions become pseudosham rites that not only are meaningless but lead to even deeper meaninglessness, the trivial and, at best, empty habit. When the rituals are authentic, then one is centered and one's sense of identity is drawn from an authentic source. For instance, the rites and ceremonies of the yearly Apache girls' puberty ritual, *na ih es*, are detailed in the myth of the female deity, Changing Woman. Once all the mythic prescriptions are followed, the young girl actually *becomes* Changing Woman for four days, during which time the girl gives the aging Changing Woman her youth and Changing Woman gives the girl her womanhood.[3] The girl's experience of the sacred thus becomes the source of her identity as an Apache woman.

Three Ritual Stages: The Plains Pipe Ceremony

Spiritually effective rites must accomplish three cumulative possibilities: purification, expansion, and identity. Purification is necessary, for that which is impure may not be united with the purity of sacred power. Expansion follows, because only that which is perfect, total, or whole can be united with absolute perfection and holiness. One must cease to be a part, an imperfect fragment; one must realize what one really is so as to expand to include the Universe within oneself. Only then, when these two conditions of purification and

Little Warrior, Sioux Holy Man, Pine Ridge, South Dakota. Photo by Joseph E. Brown.

expansion have been actualized, may one attain the final stage, in which one's identity is grounded in a union with all that is.

The sacred rites of the Plains Indian tobacco pipe, embody these possibilities. The shape of the pipe, with its stem, bowl or "heart," and foot, is identified with the human person. The purification of the pipe with sage or sweet grass before a ritual smoking is analogous to a human's own purification; the concentration on the hollow of the straight stem leading to the bowl brings the understanding that one's mind should be that straight and pure. In filling the bowl of the pipe, the leader of the ceremony holds a pinch of tobacco and points it in each of the six directions of space. Then he holds up a pinch of tobacco and says, "This is for all the wingeds of the air, this is for all the four-legged peoples of this earth, this is for all the growing peoples of this earth," and the pinch is put into the pipe. He may offer another pinch, saying, "This pinch of tobacco is for all the waters, the rivers, the lakes of this world. This is for all the thunder beings, all the powers of the universe," and so on. A grain of tobacco is also offered for the person who smokes the pipe.

When the pipe is filled, the entire universe, the totality of all that is, is encapsulated in the filled bowl. The fire that is used to light the pipe is understood to be an expression of the Great Mysterious that is the ultimate principle of all things. When the tobacco is consumed in that fire, all things are united; all things become one in the smoke that rises up to the heavens. And, since in the pipe there is a grain of tobacco identified with the one who smokes, a sacrificial communion of identity is enacted. If the smoker is aware of this principle, he or she will be helped to understand that he or she is not separate from the totality of the universe but is at one with all that is. With this understanding, the phrase *Mitakuye Oyasin*, 'we are all related,' recited by the individual or group after the smoking, takes on the deepest possible meaning.

Mythic Reenactment:
The Ojibwa Medewewin Ceremony

Initiation rites contain ritual elements similar to those in the Plains pipe ceremony, for, through the complex ritual processes of purification and expansion, the initiate is born into a new identity. Such complexity is well illustrated by the Medewewin medicine dance, or the Medicine Lodge Society of the Ojibwa-Chippewa of the Great Lakes region. These ceremonies normally occur semiannually, in late spring and early fall. Candidates seek initiation into the sacred society for a variety of reasons. Maybe they have had dream or vision experiences in retreats that indicate they should seek admission. Often they enter the society because they have become ill as a result of a transgression, such as failing to pay proper respect to a slain animal. Such persons are then instructed by the *mide* priests in the sacred lore, songs, and other requirements for entry.

During the Medewewin, the leader of the rite tells listeners that long ago, the Earth-Supernatural, also called the Shell-Covered One, pitied the humans for their vulnerability to disease and death. Shell sent Bear to ask the Great Spirit if he could give the Medewewin to the humans so that they would have long, healthy lives. The Great Spirit thought that was a very good idea, so Bear traveled the land of the Ojibwa, stopping at Lake Superior, Birch Point, Open Beach, and Flagweed Bay, and prepared the land for the Medewewin by telling the local manitos (spirits): "And now from here you will satisfy the Indian's needs when he so requests."[4] Bear laid down the sacred geography of the Medewewin, and when participants hear this story, they are reminded that the land in which they live, move, and exist is not only infused with manitos but also has the potential to heal them. When Bear's preparations were complete, Shell appeared to a young boy named Cutfoot in two visions, and he revealed the Medewewin ceremony to him. Now, patients relive this visionary experience, for, in the reenactment, there is life and healing.

The Medewewin rites are conducted within a long lodge conceived as an image of the universe. Covered with saplings and brush, the lodge contains four sacred cedar poles representing the four layers of the earth penetrated by Bear in mythic time. Since Bear's travels began in the East, the opening of the lodge faces East. Within the lodge, and guarding the doorways, are certain forms identified with animal-spirit helpers and guardians. They are the mythic beings who protect the portals into innermost being. Purification in a sweat lodge, a requirement for participation in the ceremony, is one of the initial stages of the rite. During the 1930s, some *mide* leaders bypassed the sweat ceremony. This greatly disturbed traditionalists who believed that not only would the entire Medewewin ceremony be rendered useless if the participants did not purify themselves for the manitos, but also that the manitos might seek revenge for this offense.[5] So important is the sweat that, if patients are well enough, they are instructed to build the lodge themselves.

The ceremony may last from two to eight days, depending on the degree of the society the candidates are entering. The first of these cumulative degrees is associated with aquatic animals referred to in myths of creation: the mink, otter, muskrat, or beaver. The second degree is associated with the beings of the air, an owl or a hawk, and the third degree with more powerful beings of the earth, such as the serpent or wildcat. The fourth and ultimate degree, which may be achieved in older age and which demands much time, preparation, and expense, is represented by the most powerful land animal, the bear. The initiation ceremony is led by a medicine man, who becomes Shell, the Earth Supernatural, for the duration of the ritual. His most important assistant is referred to as the Bowman, the one with the eyes at the front of the canoe, and he becomes Bear. They are supported by a string of men representing the manitos who assisted at the original Medewewin and whose power is necessary for the ceremony. At the end of this line is Steersman, who steers from the back of the canoe.

Art forms, created in the sacred manner discussed earlier, are central to the ceremony. When the priests or medicine men tell of creation and sacred migration, they use carefully incised birch bark scrolls as mnemonic aids. Patients use sticks whittled from cedar and dyed red to invite the medicine men to accept the goods they have sacrificed as payment. The origin myth tells that people first used their fingers to invite the medicine men, but then they forgot to do it. Shell grew concerned that the people would fail to do the rites properly, so he sent Bear to splinter a cedar tree and to show the people how to use the sticks. The many drums used to carry the songs and dances to the manitos also have their prototype in the origin myths. When Bear was preparing the Medewewin, he became worried that the ceremony would be too much for the people to handle. One of the manitos offered to turn himself into a drum to help the people uphold the rites. These artistic creations are of the greatest beauty, for they come from a sacred inspiration, are made in a ritual process, and are used to sustain life and harmonious relations with the manitos.

The Medewewin ceremony comes to a dramatic climax when the candidates are ritually "shot" by the priests, using an otter skin bag out of which the sacred *mi'gis*, or cowry shell, is magically propelled into the candidate, who drops to the ground, experiencing a spiritual death. The shells, manifestations of Shell, contain an essence of life so vital they are believed to reproduce in the otter skin bags. When these shells strike the patient, he or she dies to the world of sickness and confusion and is then reborn into a new world of deeper spiritual understanding. The physical experience of being shot and falling down provides a sense of immediacy to the process of spiritual rebirth. The prescribed actions of the Medewewin mean that participation is not just with the mind, or with a part of one's being, but with the totality of who one is. Also provided are means for continuity, since the patient's new life and identity find a place within the Medicine Lodge Society.

Although the Ojibwa people have had intense contacts over many centuries with Euro-American peoples and cultures, and have experienced loss of lands, new types of subsistence economies, the introduction of Christianity, and, most recently, the new, syncretistic Peyote religion of the Native American Church, not only is the Medewewin still observed, but there is evidence of increasing participation in the ceremony. Melinda Gopher, an Ojibwa woman, remarks that, "despite the fact that we've been struggling just to survive, we have done a very good job of preserving our traditions, because we relied on them so heavily." Explaining why it is essential that these rites and ceremonies are maintained, she continues, "The songs we sing in our sweats are so much more than just songs—our theological beliefs are in there, as well as our history and our connection to the Earth."[6]

Breaking through with Laughter: The Lakota Heyhokas

That these are serious, sacred rites doesn't mean that the rites do not contain some humor. Very often, right in the middle of a sacred ritual such as the opening of a sacred bundle, people may start telling funny stories. Suddenly, in this most serious context, people are laughing and holding their sides. Their laughter may seem to ridicule the rite, thus destroying it, but it does this so that the deeper truths contained within the rite can come forth and reveal themselves. It is a shattering of the structure in order to get at the essence. Among many tribes on the Northwest coast, certain rites and ceremonies cannot be started until the guests who have been invited to participate start to laugh. Once they are laughing, the ground is prepared for a real quality of participation.

In many traditional societies, the clown is the first one to break through the solemnity of a ceremony. This is accomplished essentially by two means. First, there is the element of shock. In the context of their ritual dance drama, for example, clowns among the Pueblo tribes engage in types of sexual display that are normally taboo in such societies. This causes a rupture with the ordinary everyday pattern of life by immediately catching people's attention. It shocks them out of the petty concerns and routines of daily life. Second, once that alertness has been achieved, then it becomes possible to communicate on a deeper level through the use of humor. Serious rituals or dance-dramas involve enormous concentration and great attention to minute detail. The rigors of these ceremonies demand some kind of relief, some way that what is being stated through the rites can be translated to a much deeper level, transcending the activities or the forms and motions of the rite itself. Thus, shock and humor open into another realm.

The *Heyhokas*, or clowns, of the Lakota are just one example of the many uses of humor among Native Americans. I have known several *Heyhokas*, including Black Elk. To become a *Heyhoka* or what is sometimes called a Contrary, requires a deep spiritual experience, such as an especially intense dream or, more often, a vision experience. This sacred origin is important, because it reveals that the activities of the *Heyhoka* are of a spiritual nature and are a means of transmitting spiritual truths to the larger community. A vision of the Thunder Beings, or one of their manifestations, such as the eagle, which is associated with lightning, is the most common signal for one to become a *Heyhoka*. A visit from the Thunderbirds is considered the greatest honor that can be given to a man or woman, after which the recipient may always call upon these powerful beings for assistance. This great honor, though, brings with it the greatest of obligations: to live the life of a *Heyhoka*. Lone Man, who received a vision of the Thunderbirds, explained:

> After my return to the camp, I wanted to do something to show that I realized my unworthiness of the honor given me by the thunderbirds. No one told me that I ought to do this, and yet all who dream of the thunderbirds in any of their manifestations have a deep sense of their own unworthiness. I knew that I was only an ordinary mortal and had often done wrong, yet the riders on the air had disregarded this. By appearing to me they had given me a chance to redeem myself. I wanted to make a public humiliation to show how deeply I realized my unworthiness.[7]

Immediately after the vision, the recipient performs a rite of public humiliation in which he or she dresses in tatters and paints his or her body with streaks of black and white lightening. The rite is directed by a medicine man and is looked upon with great reverence. After the rite, the *Heyhoka* takes up the burden of constantly breaking with traditional norms. The *Heyhokas* do all sorts of strange things. They do things upside down or backwards; sometimes they will pitch a tipi with the poles on the outside of the lodge covering, with the smoke flaps facing the wrong way, or with the doorway to the west instead of to the east. When they sit in the tipi, they may sit upside down, with their feet up in the air, or lying on their backs on the ground. This, of course, makes people laugh. Normally, when you enter a tipi in the Plains, you must move around it in a sunwise direction, clockwise; but the *Heyhoka* will do it the wrong way. Sometimes, instead of going in the doorway, they lift up the lodge cover at the back and crawl under. These humorous actions help shatter people's perception of, and participation in, the routines of life. To break through the habitual enables one to take some distance from oneself—to see things more objectively and, thereby, on a higher level.

Sometimes the tricks aren't so funny. I remember one story an old Lakota woman told me about a situation that made her very angry. Her husband was a *Heyhoka*, and she had just finished making a pair of decorated moccasins for him. They were in the lodge, and she tossed them to him across the fire, saying, "Here, try them on." In Lakota, that sounds very much like "Here, burn them up," and so he picked them up and threw them into the fire, destroying his nice new moccasins. She was furious. She didn't think that was very funny at all. Though it made her angry, it also may have helped her gain a greater distance from her craft work, teaching her not to become too attached to the things she made and not to forget that things are never permanent.

Black Elk used to tell a story about the *Heyhokas* who rushed out of the tipi after a little sprinkling of rain and said they saw a large puddle. With great flourish and gesticulations, they took off their clothes down to the breech cloth and got a long pole, about twenty feet long, and laid it horizontally across the puddle, which wet the pole along its length. Then they set it up vertically in order to measure the depth of the water, and said it was about twenty feet deep. So with a great deal of display, making sure everybody in camp was looking, they dove into the water—which in reality was only a few inches deep—and hit their heads hard and made everybody laugh.

Sometimes, the trick backfires in tragic ways. For example, as a *Heyhoka*, Black Elk had the right and, indeed, the obligation to do things that were amazing and unnatural. He once proclaimed that he was going to make the earth rise in front of everybody within the tipi. What he had done was place gunpowder a few inches under the surface of the earth, and, at a certain point in his ceremony, when he called on the earth to rise, he touched off the gunpowder with a cigarette. Indeed, the earth did rise, but the flareup from the gunpowder was too close to him, and it singed his eyes. From then on he was almost completely blind. No one else was hurt, but he always used to say that he had been punished for going too far in fooling people.

Very often it is evident to the outsider that there is some pragmatic explanation for these tricks, some sleight of hand. Usually that is the case, and the people are very aware of it, but they do not think the performer is a fake or a charlatan. They relate to this in a different kind of way than non-Natives would. They regard it not with suspicion but with an understanding that, however the phenomenon is accomplished, it illustrates the illusory nature of phenomena in general. Realizing this illusory nature of phenomena also helps one break through to a clearer understanding of reality.

Black Elk was always doing funny, unexpected things, which is why it was good to live with him. Something most unexpected happened on a trip we took to Denver, and, though it wasn't exactly humorous, it did show the ability of the *Heyhoka* to seize on any occasion and use it in an imaginative, unusual way. Denver in the early 1940s was not a very pleasant city; there was a great deal of racism, and we had a hard time finding a hotel that would rent a room to a Native American. When we finally found a hotel that would accept us, the room was very dingy and horrible. Black Elk felt bad about Denver and the hotel. He felt unclean and wanted a sweat bath to cleanse himself of the impurities of the city. I didn't know how this could be done in a hotel room, but the room was heated by a coal fire, and the fireplace was so old that the bricks were falling out of it. He said, "Here, let's take these loose bricks, and we'll put some more out of the chimney and heat them in the coal fire," which we did. Then we took the chairs in the room and put them in a circle, took all the bedding off the beds, and put them over the chairs to make a kind of lodge right there in the middle of the hotel room. We found an old coal scuttle, and, when the bricks were red hot, we put them in the coal scuttle, placed the scuttle in the little lodge, stripped down, and crawled in. It was good and hot in there, and we sang and prayed and smoked and sweated, and it was very good. I think that was the first time a sweat bath has ever been taken in a Denver hotel room, but that is typical of the kind of thing that happens with *Heyhokas*. The unexpected, the breaking with habitual patterns, adds a dimension to life that is very important.

Whenever there were little children around, Black Elk would do funny tricks or tell them silly stories to make them laugh. He seemed to understand that there is no access to a deeper spiritual reality without the opening force of laughter. Despite his good humor, however, there were many times in his life in which he felt terribly saddened. He thought he had never brought to full realization the task that had been imposed upon him through his vision: to mend the hoop of his nation, to bring his people together, and to make the tree of his culture flourish again. He felt he had failed in this mission. Typical of the dual nature of the *Heyhoka*, he was sorrowful, but he also loved to laugh and to make other people laugh as well.

The most sacred is often hidden in strange ways, and there is a very great wisdom concealed behind practices of the *Heyhokas*. While Shakespeare has his clowns and cinema has its comic heroes, much of Western culture has lost sight of the spiritual dimension of humor. The antics of the *Heyhoka* might well remind us that laughter can carry us into a deeply spiritual realm.

"The Earth, Its Life Am I": Navajo Chantways

The list of Native American rites and their serious and humorous dimensions is very long. But, whether the ceremony is simple or complex, they all help intensify people's experience of the sacred through time and place, language, art forms, music, and dance. It is through such ritual means that purity of being and world is sought, that fragmentation gives way to relationship, and human and world become one. In all that I have tried to speak of in such a brief fashion, we have expressions of this special quality among traditional peoples that could be called oneness of experience: a lack of dichotomizing, a unity in the word and in the visual image. One can draw examples from all Native American cultures to reinforce such interpretation, but one final illustration I will use is that of the sandpaintings from the Navajo chantway healing rituals.

Central to the Navajo view of the world and reality is the understanding that everything exists in pairs that complement each other and belong together. The natural urge of humans, deities, and nature is toward *hózhó*, beauty, long-life, and goodness, but the complement of *hózhó* also exists. If living in balance and health is goodness, then living in disorder and sickness is evil. The world for the Navajo is a potentially dangerous place, for there are many ways in which order can break down. Disregard for ritual practices or contact with snakes, ants, lightning, ghosts, foul weather, and especially witchcraft can cause illness, as does excess in any action, such as weaving, drinking, or concentration. Attempts to master nature are also disruptive, for the Navajo believe that, while humans can restore nature, they can never overpower it.

Fortunately, evil can be dispelled and balance restored through the lengthy chantway ceremonies passed on from mythic time. Through prayer, song, and sandpainting, the Navajo can coerce the *Yei* (deities, or Holy People) into manifesting themselves at the ceremony and reestablishing order. The Navajo see little distinction between the *Yei*, animals, natural forces, and humans, because they were all created from similar substances. Thus, when the Navajo need the assistance of the *Yei* to be cured, they do not appeal to them in supplication or subservience. They simply go through the necessary steps to enlist their presence within the healing ritual. Once the *Yei* are present, the patient identifies with them and is able to draw upon their power to become healthy again. In the Navajo system of healing, like cures like. A patient in need of rejuvenation becomes Changing Woman, who is continually restored to youth and beauty. A person sick from a snake bite becomes Snake; a person stricken by trickery or deceit becomes Coyote. Even though Snake and Coyote are considered evil because they cause illness and disruption, the Navajo recognize that all things, even the *Yei*, have the capacity for both good and evil. Evil can be transformed into goodness and order within the ritual ceremony.

The *Yei* will be compelled to come and identify with the patient only if the ceremony follows the prototypical chantway revealed in mythic time. The following quotation demonstrates the necessity of precision and exactitude:

> You must be careful about introducing things into ceremonies. One chanter thought that he could do this. He held a Night Chant. He wanted more old people so he had the dancers cough and dance as old people. He also wanted an abundance of potatoes so he painted potatoes on the dancers' bodies. He desired that there should be a great deal of food so he had the

dancers break wind and vomit through their masks to make believe that they had eaten a great deal. They surely got their reward. Through the coughing act a great many of the people got whooping cough and died. In the second change many of the people got spots on their bodies like potatoes only they were measles, sores, and smallpox. In the part where they asked for all kinds of food, a lot died of diarrhea, vomiting and stomach aches. This chanter thought that he had the power to change things but everyone found out that he was wrong. It was the wrong thing to do and today no one will try to start any new ceremonies. Today we do not add anything. . . .[8]

Each element in the chantway must be executed with utmost care, including the consecration of the hogan, the laying out of prayer sticks, and the many purifying sweat, emetic, and vomiting ceremonies the patient must undergo. Together with the proper songs, the careful imitation of the original chantways recreates the time when harmony prevailed. Navajo songs and words have a generative power that brings thought into being so that the telling of the origin myths and the repetition of mythic prayers actually propel the participants into the timelessness of mythic time. Invoking the four holy mountains of the Navajo world and describing the sacred landscape allow mythic time to take place. Every chantway recreates the world, as this sweathouse song from the creation myth illustrates:

The earth has been laid down, the earth has been laid down
The earth has been laid down, it has been made.
The earth spirit has been laid down
It is covered over with the growing things, it has been laid down
Sahanahray Bekayhozhon have been laid down
The earth has been laid down, it has been made . . .
The mountains have been lad down, the mountains have been laid down
The mountains have been laid down, they have been made.
The mountain spirits have been laid down
They are covered over with all the animals, they have been laid down.[9]

The world was made in beauty and harmony, the very state that has been disrupted. By ritually recreating the world, the chantway can restore the original balance, which will contribute to the healing of the patient. The following chant invokes the sacred beauty that all are striving for:

> The Earth is beautiful
> The Earth is beautiful
> The Earth is beautiful
> Below, the East, the Earth, its face toward East
> The top of its head is beautiful
> The soles of its feet, they are beautiful
> Its feet, they are beautiful
> Its legs, they are beautiful
> Its body, it is beautiful
> Its chest, it is beautiful
> Its breast, it is beautiful
> Its head-feather, it is beautiful
> The Earth is beautiful.[10]

The invocation of mythic time and the world's original harmony compel the *Yei* to become present. The patient experiences an expanded world and is ready to become identified with their power through the sandpaintings.

Sandpaintings, made from colored sand and pollen, are always of great aesthetic beauty. The purpose and reality of the sandpainting, however, is not in the finished product, which must be ritually destroyed because the power it contains may get out of control outside the ritual context. Rather, its meaning is both in the presence of sacred natural materials used and, above all, in the ritual processes of its creation. The painting is not a symbol of some meaning or power; rather, the power is present in it. At a certain moment during the ceremony, the ill person sits at the center of a sandpainting so that, by actual identification with sacred substances and with the graphic depiction of a controlled and balanced cosmos, harmony may be restored to one who has temporarily suffered loss of relationship and therefore of identity. The singer takes some of the painted image and presses it to the body of the ill person, to emphasize this element of identity. Through the connection established with sacred power, a relationship unfolds between the patient and the world around him or her:

> The Earth is looking at me; she is looking up at me
> I am looking down on her
> I am happy, she is looking at me
> I am happy, I am looking at her.

> The Sun is looking at me; he is looking down on me
> I am looking up at him
> I am happy, he is looking at me
> I am happy, I am looking at him.

> The Black Sky is looking at me; he is looking down on me
> I am looking up at him
> I am happy, he is looking at me
> I am happy, I am looking at him.[11]

Reciprocity, an expression of harmony, is created, and the patient knows that he or she will never be alone or isolated from the world because he or she is a part of it. This is illustrated in a chant I learned from a Navajo elder:

> The mountains, I become part of it . . .
> The herbs, the fir tree, I become part of it.
> The morning mists, the clouds, the gathering waters,
> I become part of it.
> The wilderness, the dew drops, the pollen . . .
> I become part of it.

By replacing the patient within the order of things, a perfect rhythm between the human and the universe is created. Once harmony, or *hozhoni*, is restored, the patient transcends being a part and becomes identified with unity of all that it is:

> Hozhoni, hozhoni, hozhoni
> Hozhoni, hozhoni, hozhoni.
> The Earth, its life am I, hozhoni, hozhoni
> The Earth, its feet are my feet, hozhoni, hozhoni
> The Earth, its legs are my legs, hozhoni, hozhoni

The Earth, its body is my body, hozhoni, hozhoni
The Earth, its thoughts are my thoughts, hozhoni, hozhoni
The Earth, its speech is my speech, hozhoni, hozhoni
The Earth, its down-feathers are my down-feathers, hozhoni, hozhoni.[12]

In the Navajo tradition, power is generated at the center and radiates out to the whole universe. Having been placed at the center, the patient is restored to harmony, and harmony ripples out to all, for, as the chant expresses, we are not separate but are one.

NOTES

Chapter One

1. Peter Nabokov, *Indian Running* (Santa Barbara: Capra Press, 1981).
2. Jane Katz, ed., *I Am the Fire of Time* (New York: Dutton, 1977), p. 162.

Chapter Two

1. Carl Sweezy, "We Counted Time by Sleeps," in *Native Heritage,* Arlene Hirschfelder, ed. (New York: Macmillan, 1995), p. 174.
2. Florence Kenney, "Men and Women Lived with the Seasons," in *Messengers of the Wind: Native American Women Tell Their Life Stories,* Jane Katz, ed. (New York: Ballantine, 1995), p. 43.
3. Esther Nahgahnub, "They're Trying to Sell Our Treaties," in *Messengers,* Jane Katz, ed., p. 239.
4. Arthur Amiotte, "The Call to Remember," *Parabola,* 17, no. 3 (Fall 1992), p. 32.
5. Richard Nelson, *Make Prayers to the Raven* (Chicago: University of Chicago Press, 1983), p. 175.
6. Vi Hilbert, "The Spirit Takes Care of Us," in *Messengers,* Jane Katz, ed., p. 244.

Chapter Three

1. Sandy Johnson, ed., *The Book of Elders* (San Francisco: Harper San Francisco, 1994), p. 127.
2. N. Scott Momday, *The Names* (New York: Harper & Row, 1976).
3. Virgina Poole, "You Take Care of the Land, and It Takes Care of You," in *Messengers,* Jane Katz, ed., p. 182.
4. Conversation with Marcia Pablo, September 1995.

5. Keith Basso, *Western Apache Language and Culture: Essays in Linguistic Anthropology* (Albuquerque: University of New Mexico, 1996). All direct quotations relating to the Western Apache in this section are also taken from this volume.

6. Klara Bonsack Kelley and Harris Francis, *Navajo Sacred Places* (Bloomington: Indiana University Press, 1994), pp. 68–70.

7. Ibid., pp. 122, 199.

8. Ibid., pp. 200–201.

9. Karl Luckert, *Navajo Mountain and Rainbow Bridge Religion* (Flagstaff: Museum of Northern Arizona, 1977), p. 41.

10. Kelley and Francis, *Navajo Sacred Places*, p. 42.

11. Ibid., p. 30.

12. Conversation with Don Good Voice, December 1995. All other quotations from Don Good Voice are from the same conversation.

13. When the National Trust for Historic Preservation added the Sweet Grass Hills to its 1993 annual list of Most Endangered Historic Sites, it noted that the Hills had been used as a sacred site for 12,000 years.

14. Chere Jiusto and Dave Schwab, *National Register of Historic Places Multiple Property Documentation Form*, U.S. Department of the Interior, National Park Services, NPS Forms 10-900-a (1991), Section E, p. 13.

15. Conversation with Pat Chief Stick, Chippewa-Cree tribal elder, in March 1996.

16. Justo and Schwab, *National Register of Historic Places Multiple Property Documentation Form*, Section F, p. 6.

17. Johnson, *The Book of Elders*, p. 50.

18. Joseph Epes Brown, *The Sacred Pipe* (Norman: Oklahoma University Press, 1953), p. 34.

19. Arthur Amiotte, "The Road to the Center," in *I Become Part of It*, D. M. Dooling and Paul Jordan Smith, eds. (New York: Parabola Books, 1989), p. 254.

Chapter Four

Note: The epigraph is from Knud Rasmussen, *The Netsilik Eskimo: Social Like and Spiritual Culture* (Copenhagen: Gyldendalske Baghandel, Nordisk Forlag, 1931), p. 320.

1. Robert Williamson, *Eskimo Underground: Socio-Cultural Change in the Central Canadian Arctic* (Upsala: Almquist & Wiksell, 1974), p. 23.

2. Ibid., pp. 23–24.

3. N. Scott Momaday, *The Names* (New York: Harper & Row, 1976).

4. Carole Anne Heart Looking Horse, "Our Cathedral Is the Black Hills," in *Messengers*, Jane Katz, ed., p. 293.

5. Gary Witherspoon, *Language and Art in the Navajo Universe* (Ann Arbor: University of Michigan Press, 1981), p. 31.

6. Gladys Reichard, *Navaho Religion, A Study of Symbolism* (Princeton, N.J.: Princeton University Press, 1990), p. 269.

7. A. Irving Hallowell, "Ojibwa Ontology, Behavior, and World View," in *Culture in History: Essays in Honor of Paul Radin*, Stanley Diamond, ed. (New York: Published for Brandeis University by Columbia University Press, 1960).

8. N. Scott Momday, "The Power and Beauty of Language," in *Native Heritage*, Arlene Hirschfelder, ed. (New York: Macmillan, 1995), p. 73.

9. Ann Renker, "Knowledge Is Not Available to Just Anyone," in *Native Heritage*, Arlene Hirschfelder, ed., p. 125.

10. Susie Yellowtail, *Susie Walking Bear Yellowtail: A Life Story*, forthcoming manuscript, Marina Brown Weatherly, ed. (copyright by editor).

11. Kenneth Lincoln, *Native American Renaissance* (Berkeley: University of California Press, 1983), p. 74.

12. Charles Alexander Eastman (Oheyesa), *The Soul of the Indian* (Boston: Houghton Mifflin, 1911), p. 34.

13. Yellowtail, manuscript, Marian Brown Weatherly, ed.

14. Rodney Frey, ed., *Stories That Make the World* (Norman: University of Oklahoma Press, 1995), p. 171.

15. Kah-ge-ga-gah-bowh (George Copway) "Ojibway Lgends," in *Native Heritage*, Arlene Hirschfelder, ed., p. 135.

16. Frey, ed., *Stories That Make the World*, p. 149.

17. Yellowtail, manuscript, Marina Brown Weatherly, ed.

18. Dennis Tedlock, "Toward the Restoration of the Word," in *alcheringa/ethnopoetics* 1975, vol. 1, no. 2, p. 128.

19. Leslie Marmon Silko, "Stories Have a Life of Their Own," in *Native Heritage*, Arlene Hirschfelder, ed., p. 147.

20. Tedlock, "Toward the Restoration of the Word," p. 126.

21. Frey, ed., *Stories That Make the World*, p. 176.

22. Ibid., p. 176.

Chapter Five

1. Herbert Spiden, *Translated Songs of the Tewa* (New York: Brooklyn Museum, 1933), p. 94.

2. Gary Witherspoon, *Language and Art in the Navajo Universe* (Ann Arbor: University of Michigan Press, 1977), p. 152.

3. Barre Toelken, "A Circular World: The Vision of Navajo Crafts," *Parabola*, 1, no. 1 (Winter 1976), p. 33.

4. Ananda Coomaraswamy, *Figures of Speech or Figures of Thought* (London: Luzac, 1946), p. 28.

5. Tom Hill and Richard Hill, Sr., eds., *Creation's Journey* (Washington: Smithsonian Insitution Press, 1994), p. 108.

6. Peter Furst and Jill Furst, *North American Indian Art* (New York: Rizzoli, 1982), p. 147.

7. Knud Rasmussen, *Intellectual Culture of the Iglulik Eskimos, Report of the Fifth Thule Expedition, 1921–24*, vol. 7, no. 1 (Copenhagen: Gyldendalske Boghandel, Nordisk Forlag, 1929), p. 114.

8. Frances Densmore, "Teton Sioux Music," *Bureau of American Ethnology Bulletin* 61 (1918), p. 184.

9. Joseph Epes Brown, *The Sacred Pipe* (Norman: University of Oklahoma Press, 1953), pp. 31–32.

10. Densmore, "Teton Sioux Music," p. 178.

11. Ted Brasser, "Wolf Collar, the Shaman as Artist," in *Stones, Bones, and Skins*, Anne Trueblood Brodzky, Rose Danesewich, and Nick Johnson, eds. (Toronto: Society for Art Publication, 1977), p. 39.

12. Dave Coolidge and Mary Coolidge, *The Navajo* (Cambridge, Mass.: Riverside Press, 1930), pp. 88–89.

13. Aileen O'Bryon, *The Dine Origin Myths of the Navajo Indians* (Washington, D.C.: Smithsonian Insititution, 1956), p. 56.

14. Franciscan Fathers, *An Ethnologic Dictionary of the Navajo Language* (St. Michaels, Ariz.: St. Michael's Press, 1910), p. 353.

15. Ibid., p. 222.

16. Ibid., p. 222.

17. David McAllester, *Navajo Creation Chants* (Cambridge, Mass.: Peabody Museum of Harvard University, no date), p. 12.

18. Gary Witherspoon, *Language and Art in the Navajo Universe* (Ann Arbor: University of Michigan Press, 1977), p. 151.

19. Susie Lindbergh, "A Navajo Weaver's Life and Art," unpublished paper, quoting Malinda Elliot, "Exploring a Tradition: Navajo Rugs, Classic and Contemporary," *Fiberarts* 2, no. 3 (May-June 1984), p. 34.

Chapter Six

Note: The epigraph is from T. C. McLuhan, ed., *Touch the Earth* (New York: Outerbridge & Dienstfrey, 1971), p. 23.

1. Ronnie Farley, *Women of the Native Struggle* (New York: Orion Books, 1993) p. 116.

2. Peter Nabokov, "America as Holy Land," *North Dakota Quarterly* (Autumn 1980) vol. 48, no. 4, p. 11.

3. Virginia Poole, "You Take Care of the Land and It Takes Care of You," in Jane Katz, ed., *Messengers of the Wind: Native American Women Tell Their Life Stories* (New York: Ballantine Books, 1995), p. 178.

4. Cf. Arthur Amiotte, "Our Other Selves: The Lakota Dream Experience," *Parabola* (Spring, 1982) 7, no. 2, p. 27.

5. Ibid., p. 30.

6. Cf. Clark Wisler, "The Whirlwind and the Elk in the Mythology of the Dakota," *Journal of American Folk-lore,* vol. 18, no. LXVIII (1905), p. 258.

7. J. R. Walker, "The Sun Dance and Other Ceremonies of the Oglala Division of the Teton Dakota," *Anthropological Papers of the American Museum of Natural History* 16, part 2 (1917), p. 152.

8. Joseph Epes Brown, *The Sacred Pipe* (Norman: University of Oklahoma Press, 1953), p. 115.

9. Knud Rasmussen, *Intellectual Culture of the Iglulik Eskimos* (Copenhagen: Gyldendalske Boghandel, Nordisk Forlag, 1929), p. 119.

10. Peter Nabokov, "Vision Quests of Crow Women," *Indian Notes* 10, no. 3 (Summer 1974), p. 82.

11. Frances Densmore, "Teton Sioux Music," *Bulletin of the Bureau of American Ethnology* 61 (1918), p. 71.

12. Sandy Johnson, ed., *The Book of Elders* (San Francisco: Harper San Francisco, 1994), p. 26.

13. Richard Nelson, *Make Prayers to the Raven* (Chicago: University of Chicago Press, 1983), p. 21.

14. Ibid., pp. 24–25.

15. Ibid., p. 24.

16. Fran James, "People Cared About One Another," in Jane Katz, ed., *Messengers*, p. 47.

17. Margot Astrov, ed., *American Indian Prose and Poetry* (New York: Capricorn Books, 1972), p. 281.

18. Elisabeth Tooker, ed., *Native North American Spirituality of the Eastern Woodlands* (New York: Paulist Press, 1979), p. 63.

19. Carole Anne Heart Looking Horse, "Our Cathedral Is the Black Hills," in *Messengers,* Jane Katz, ed., p. 297.

20. Astrov, ed., *American Indian Prose and Poetry,* p. 85.

21. D'Arcy McNickle, *They Came Here First* (Philadelphia: J. B. Lippincott, 1949), p. 264.

22. *Target Tabloid,* March 9, 1962.

23. Janet McCloud, "You Defend What's Sacred to You," in *Messengers,* Jane Katz, ed., p. 282.

24. Rasmussen, *Intellectual Culture of the Iglulik Eskimos,* p. 56.

25. K. J. Butler, "My Uncle Went to the Moon," in *Stones, Bones, and Skins,* Anne Trueblood Brodzky, Rose Danesewich, and Nick Johnson, eds. (Toronto: Society for Art Publication, 1977), p. 122.

26. Rasmussen, *Intellectual Culture of the Iglulik Eskimos,* p. 129.

27. A. Grove Day, *The Sky Clears, Poetry of the American Indians* (Lincoln: University of Nebraska, 1951), p. 41.

Chapter Seven

1. Kenneth Lincoln, *Native American Renaissance* (Berkeley: University of California Press, 1983), p. 150.

2. Elisabeth Tooker, ed., *Native American Spirituality of the Eastern Woodlands* (New York: Paulist Press, 1979), p. 271.

3. Inés Talamantez, "Dance and Ritual in the Study of Native American Religious Traditions," in *Native American Quarterly* (Fall/Winter, 1982), vol. 6, nos. 3–4, p. 345.

4. Ruth Landes, *Ojibwa Religion and the Midewiwin* (Madison: University of Wisconsin Press, 1968), p. 100.

5. Ibid., p. 118.

6. Ronnie Farley, *Women of the Native Struggle* (New York: Orion Books, 1993), p. 46.

7. Francis Densmore, "Teton Sioux Music," *Bulletin of the Bureau of American Ethnology* 61 (1918), p. 164.

8. Cldye Kluchohn and Dorothea Leighton, "The Navaho View of Life," in *Man Makes Sense*, Eugene Hammel, ed. (Boston: Little, Brown, 1970), p. 345.

9. Hosteen Klah, recorded by Mary C. Wheelwright, *Navajo Creation Myth* (Santa Fe: Museum of Navajo Ceremonial Art, 1942), p. 136.

10. Ibid., p. 161.

11. Ibid., p. 149.

12. Ibid., p. 142.

References to figures are italicized.

134

139

DATE DUE

DE 21 '02			
AG 28 '03			
MR 14 '04			
MY 30 '04			
JA 24 '05			
AP 16 '08			
FEB 2 3 2011			

#47-0108 Peel Off Pressure Sensitive